nocturne with the invisible shepherd // or the book of noah

the boys were the brain of the herd.
but the brain stood nowhere close

to its head: instead the lambs led
the charge across the pasture of ash

from tyres burnt to protest the arrest
of the town's rebel cleric.

the dry grass brown and thirsty for
prodigal rains at the fringes of the sand

that led nowhere towards an active brook.
then came their sluggish mothers,

sheep coerced by their own partners—
rams smelling of sex and botched sacrifices

bearing horns that have subdued grudges
and battle cries every day—like my country

on the eve of the civil war. then came
the chubby cows lifting their tired

boots like a python. it was not written
but the serpent's punishment was total

VOLUME 52.1, FALL 2019

EDITORIAL BOARD

Editor
Keith Lee Morris

Managing Editor
Elizabeth Stansell

Poetry Editor
Jillian Weise

Fiction Editor
Nic Brown

Fiscal Analyst
Susan Chastain

Associate Editors
Sarah Cooper
Melissa Dugan
Dan Leach
John Pursley
Geveryl Robinson
John Saylor
Will Stockton

Assistant Editors
Wesley Kapp
Tara Lenertz
Blake Steen

FRIENDS OF *THE SCR*

The editorial board wishes to acknowledge the generous support of our patrons: Wayne K. Chapman and Janet M. Manson; John Idol, Jr.; Ronald Moran; and Dick and Doris Calhoun.

The South Carolina Review is published by Clemson University Press
801 Strode Tower, Clemson, SC 29634
© 2019 Clemson University ISSN 0038-3163

Typeface: Minion Pro
Cover Art: *Miles Below,* 2019, Kaitlin Francis

EDITORIAL CORRESPONDENCE

The Editor, *The South Carolina Review*
Center for Electronic and Digital Publishing
Clemson University, Strode Tower, Box 340522
Clemson, SC 29634-0522
Tel. (864) 656-3151 (864) 656-5399   Fax (864) 656-1345

SUBSCRIPTION INFORMATION*

Individual	*Institutional*
Single Copy $17	Single Copy $17
One-year subscription $28	One-year subscription $33
Two-year subscription $40	Two-year subscription $47
Three-year subscription $54	Three-year subscription $61

*Including postage and handling in the US only. Add an additional $10 per annum for subscribers outside the United States and Canada.

Subscribe and order copies from our web site
http://www.clemson.edu/cedp/cudp/scr/scrintro.htm

The South Carolina Review is indexed in the *MLA International Bibliography, Humanities International Complete, Index to Periodical Fiction,* and *Book Review Index. SCR* belongs to the Council of Editors of Learned Journals and the Council of Literary Magazines and Presses. Content from *SCR* 37.1 onward is also available vis ProQuest's online database (http://www.proquest.com).

Entered as fourth-class mail at Clemson, SC 29634-0522

CONTENTS

amputation for the sin that caught him
red-handed. father hides his grip so well

you wouldn't see the tumour i almost
thought he had nothing to hide inside

like my language would lie to you.
the harmattan haze would make you

believe everything you do not see:
my father a silhouette painted from steam.

the last time he came out of a tomb,
he brought a horsewhip to put the calves

in line. we mooed gently into his correction
although this poem will step out of line.

prayer slid under the study door

don't leave me here for hours with my glass cats shut up in the curtained room

don't leave me here moonlight on the gritty roof

don't leave me here overlooking the long backyard bordered by thorny raspberry
and crumbling garages

hulks of rusted cars standing on cinder blocks like the huge shed hulls of insects

don't leave me alone flies scattered lifeless across the sill

don't leave me alone the slanted trees

don't leave me alone all I have are the slanted trees

will you meet me there? one day?

please meet me at the slanted trees

please let me touch the sleeves of your sweater

let me roll the rough poppyseed paste up in dough for you

let me give you a drink of canteen water

please I know I ransacked your desk

I know I broke into your studio and rifled through your condoms

I know I pulled the guts out of your mix tape I know I shredded a book of poems
    in revenge

I know I read your secrets scotch taped to the wall

but please the plums are rotting in the frosty grass

and the one star's a shiny metal splinter in the black heel of the sky

and this house isn't burning but help me out of the high window like it was

walk with me just across this orchard take my elbow like we're not meant to be
    alone

S
C
R

Sugar Talk

When was the last time that the two of them, Brenda and Louisa, had sat around a hotel breakfast table together? What funeral, what wedding? Louisa, pinching her left earring closer to the lobe, shrugged and shook her head. Brenda raised her eyes to the ceiling, considering, blinking sleepily—her blue eyes moist, as they often were. Neither could remember. They had gathered this time to visit their brother Wyatt, recovering in the hospital. Open-heart surgery. What they didn't—couldn't—ask each other: if not their brother, this time, then which one of them, the next? A fruitless calculus. There was no telling. The sticky web of familial obligation in Death's antechamber, the difficulty of distinguishing fly from spider. What manner of release awaited each of them? And to whom the misfortune, the privilege—the exultant betrayal—of first departure from those kindred bones and sinews?

Marvin, new loafers squeaking faintly, returned from the breakfast buffet; Louisa pulled her husband's chair out for him. Grave with concentration, solicitous, he set two plates of breakfast sweets—a glistening sticky bun for Louisa, crumb cake for Brenda—on the tiled table.

Above the whir of air conditioning, the television murmured urgently of midweek thunderstorms. The air in the breakfast room thickened with the aroma of waffle batter crisping in its iron.

Brenda sighed and settled into her chair—a godsend, she told herself, not to be shuttling off to the hospital first thing in the morning. They had stayed at Wyatt's bedside through the evening yesterday. She could see that Marvin didn't like being there, at the hospital, though her sister—Marvin was Louisa's second husband—didn't seem to notice. Marvin had just now sloshed a bit of coffee over the rim of his cup; Brenda passed him a paper hotel napkin. His hands sometimes trembled, Brenda had detected these last two days, when he was holding a book or a glass.

"Seems to agree with Wyatt, doesn't it?" Brenda said. "Those batting eyelashes and all that sugar talk. Making the nurses fall in love with him."

She sat up straighter, graced suddenly with a retrieval: "Gloria! That's her name—that's the nurse who told me that Wyatt asked her for a nip of whisky." She shook her head and closed her eyes and allowed a smile, imagining. "I say Gloria's the nicest of the bunch," she said, opening her eyes again.

She saw now that Louisa had taken a lipstick out of her purse and, dabbing color on, wasn't listening. And a perfectly good sticky bun just sitting there on Louisa's plate, going to waste. Forever watching her figure, Louisa. Brenda had always been apple-cheeked, gathering crumbs with soft fingertips, a friend to all, absorbing confessions. Though never Louisa's confessions; Louisa kept things to herself. "Don't you think that Gloria's the nicest? Weeza?"

I may as well be talking to myself in the hotel mirror, Brenda thought.

"There sure are a lot of them, those nurses," said Louisa. Brenda had been saying something about the different nurses, she wasn't sure what, but no doubt it was a compliment, an admission of empathy, the pardoning of some small but irritating administrative bungle. That was Brenda for you. Spilling bright sentiment, a pond after an April storm. "They're hard to tell apart. There's the one with the purple nails," Louisa said, adjusting the knot of her cream silk scarf. "And then there's that young one, with all those little braids and the Caribbean accent."

She'd rather have gone for a walk, frankly, but her sister had insisted on breakfast all together.

The hotel breakfast room was full of families; each one seemed to have at least six children. Otherwise it was elderly couples. Stooped, wrinkled, tremulous, it was hard to tell which member of each couple was waiting to check into the hospital nearby. A knobby-kneed boy stalked past, clinging grimly to his glass of orange juice. If I take even one bite of that sticky bun, Louisa was thinking, crossing her feet beneath the chair, I've as good as eaten the whole thing. Marvin had brought it to the table for her—Marvin, who should know better.

Wyatt flirting for whisky, from the hospital bed. Well. Marvin could believe it. Wyatt had always been impish, and especially when it came to drink, for as long as Marvin had known him—twelve years now, Marvin calculated, turning the empty coffee cup on its saucer. At Christmas: red-tipped ears, florid nose, teasing his sisters, performing pratfalls.

With Philip it's different, thought Marvin. Philip, a punishing sort of drunk. I almost lost it with him that once. (Marvin pulling Philip by his legs out of his tangle-sheeted, musty bed; Philip falling, Philip rising fist-first at Marvin, veins popping, bellowing.) Almost got my .45 that time. For both of us. That must have been the fall of Philip's senior year, with Jeannie dying the summer before. Each playing their thankless role: Philip the motherless son, Marvin the widowed father.

And after that the brown-fog years, five in all, before Louisa stood there next to Marvin, hair tucked behind her ears, wearing that yellow dress and holding the nosegays to the side as she leaned in for the kiss. The front pews full of witnesses smiling and nodding, flush-faced Wyatt dabbing his eyes with the rest of them. (That rubber tree under the closest window, beside the vent—Marvin noticed now—was real; you could tell from how its leaves shone, plump with water, a living skin. Its leaves bobbed shyly in a rush of cool air.)

He had never told Louisa about that one time, the time he almost lost it. But Philip was doing all right now. Sober for one whole year. Tell him how proud you are, Louisa had been saying lately; tell him.

"The insurance won't pay for Wyatt much longer," said Louisa. Oh Brenda, Brenda, clanking your spoon against the inside of your bowl, hunting for dregs of raisin bran. For the love of God, please stop. How like their mother Brenda had become. The three of them would need to talk to Wyatt about his situation, and today. Has this occurred to anyone but me? she thought. Of course it hasn't. Things are healing up nicely, that's what the doctor said yesterday. And it was what the doctors said that mattered. Never mind the nurses. Louisa had had Marvin call Philip that morning, while she was in the shower, to tell him they'd be back home by Friday night at the latest.

Louisa stacked her water glass into Marvin's now. If he would just clear away the breakfast plates already, she wouldn't have to keep telling herself not to eat the sticky bun. "He's sweeter to a bunch of strangers than he is to me," she said. She had never said that about Wyatt till then, had never even thought the thing. But it was true. Flushed with sudden anger, she put a hand to her hot cheek. Small Wyatt and smaller Brenda across the dinner table from her, all those years ago, exchanging sideways glances, trading silent oaths of fealty—Louisa watching them array themselves against her.

"They're not really strangers though, the nurses. At this point. Are they?" said Brenda. "Did you try this, Weeza? Some kind of crumb cake. It's good. And I've got an extra fork, somehow."

"You know I don't have a sweet tooth," said Louisa.

Soon she and Marvin would be home again. Friday at the latest. What she hadn't expected was missing her stepson's loping gait, his rueful half-smile.

She glanced at her wristwatch, at its rising arc of silhouetted sun: nearly nine o'clock. By the time the alarm goes off, she was thinking to herself—as she pushed the sticky bun away, she clinked her plate against Brenda's accidentally—by the time the sky is streaking white, it's too late. Philip hadn't overslept yet in the months he'd been sober and living with her and Marvin. But he had come close. And if he wakes up late and misses his bus and loses a day of work, and then another, and another? How long before it all unravels?

What you have to do, she kept telling Marvin, over and over, is have Philip set the alarm for fifteen minutes *before* he really needs to get up. It was Marvin's to say, not hers; she wasn't going to intervene. She stirred before dawn lately, listening for it, one ear still cradled warmly by the pillow: the bleating herald from down the hall, brighter than a heartbeat. Honey, honey, you are still alive. Wake up.

These Uncharted Wilds

when she did it
I was a little amazed at the ease of it all
so ready
already playing dead

she was begging
for it, made me feel like
the strongest man in the world
she asked me
to lie back
to do it,

end it all.

how could it be murder
in these uncharted wilds
that can't offer a true hiding place
all that nothing
trying to burst out of her
even before
there was a knife

Along the Bay

I miss the birds, mostly
I miss the animals almost as much
coexisting peacefully beneath the museums
dolphins wandering, lost, at the shallow end of the water

but I don't miss the people
tobacco-chewing alcoholics
end-of-the-world placards
if all the people disappeared
I might just move back.

Marcyland

Twelve tree houses perched along the lip of the lake where Marcy gathered flowers for the new hired help. Summer tore through the town. There were steamboats and Elvis impersonators and the crawl of a parade. Ice cream cones grew multiple heads. Marcy's fingers were stained with dirt. She loved this time of year. Summers in Lake George meant more live music in bars and more strangers in the trees.

Marcy was twelve and full of a longing she couldn't understand. Fables were in her genes. She imagined herself as Athena and Rapunzel. Some days she was a high priestess or keeper of a golden egg. She saw herself wandering vast lonely corridors lined with secret knowledge. In these stories, nothing bad ever happened to clever girls, and Marcy was clever.

Her mother Gloria was washing vegetables in the kitchen, her hair so long she couldn't keep it from the faucet's stream. She was beautiful but modest. Every time Marcy complimented her, she said, "Only in Marcyland."

Dalia, the new housekeeper, had arrived a few hours earlier than expected. Twenty-one, she lived in New York City where she worked at a string of temp agencies to fund her performing arts career. Her family had vacationed at the resort when she was a child. When she reached out to Gloria for a summer job, she was more than happy to take her on.

In her imagination, Dalia was a young woman who ate like a girl from the country, yet guzzled coffee and danced inside translucent installations. She'd pierced her nose and wore a heap of makeup. Her expression was secretive and informed but not unkind. Her lips were full, her forehead stamped with curls. She hailed from a neighborhood called Bushwick.

Gloria rushed from the kitchen to hug her, then gestured to the tree house in the big red oak. Halfway up the stairs, Dalia looked over her shoulder and smiled. "Wait a minute," she said. "Is that Marcy?"

Marcy nodded.

"Last I saw you," Dalia said, "you could barely talk."

Marcy said nothing.

"Well, see you around," Dalia said.

That night Marcy read a story about a wizard dressed as a beggar who went to the houses of pretty girls. At a house that belonged to three beautiful sisters, when the oldest handed the wizard a piece of bread, he carried her away in his basket, promising she could have whatever her heart desired. The rooms in his house shone with silver and gold, all but one of which she could enter. One day he set out on a journey and left her with a key and an egg. Curiosity at last having got the better of her, the sister entered the forbidden chamber, egg in hand, to find it filled with women hewn to pieces. She dropped the egg into a pool of blood, but couldn't wipe it clean. Again and again the bloody spots returned. The next day the wizard saw the blood on the egg and knew the sister had disobeyed him. "Since you have gone into the room against my will," he said, "you will go back into it now against your own." Then he cut off the girl's head and threw her into the chamber with the rest.

Marcy lived upstairs in the resort's office, her home. Her room faced the lake and the houses in towering trees. There were few visitors that summer. Their lights were out. Dalia's light flickered from above. It was as though the tree peered at Marcy and winked.

She heard a noise and went down to the kitchen. In the moonlight, a man was kissing her mother. The man smiled, and Marcy stiffened. An unerring knowledge pulsed through her. She'd never felt anything like it.

"There she is," the man said.

"Marcy," Gloria said, "you should be in bed. There's a lot of work tomorrow."

Marcy saw the man's arm snake around Gloria's waist. "Your mother's right, Marcy. You work too hard. Get some sleep."

As if hexed, her eyelids grew heavy. She longed for night and its better dreams.

"Your mother," the man said, "tells me that sometimes you wear a crown of flowers in your hair. Will I get to see it, Marcy?" She thought of her green wire crown of plastic baby's breath and roses. Her scalp prickled. "To see both of you in that crown," the man said, kissing Gloria's head, "would be like a dream."

After lunch, Marcy had time for a dip. She ran barefoot in a white bikini covered in starfish. Speedboats were humming across the lake. She stopped before the tree houses, paralyzed. The bikini no longer fit her like it had. The bottom pinched her hips. Her waist looked indented. Her chest thundered when she moved. She took a long breath. Everyone could see.

The man walked toward her from the lake. He wore swim trunks but his hair and skin were dry. She saw, in his eyes, shades of dangerous uncertainty. It was as if she were expected to help him somehow, like she had helped her mother for as long as she could remember. She felt peculiar, dizzy. Not all was right. The man slipped his fingers into the elastic of his trunks and took out his phone. He saw the look on Marcy's face and howled.

"You thought!" he said. "You actually thought!"

He stepped toward her. She pushed him, and his phone fell in the water. He swore and called her the name of a place inside her. She imagined this place covered in a breathing web of lace. He fished his phone from the water. She dove in and swam until there was nothing but the blurred image of him on the shore. She lay on her back and sighed. The sky curved above. She let the sun stream down her body. She was aware now of how she swam. There was a fullness to her that swelled underwater. She ran her hands over her skin and fell in love with what she felt. She thought of Dalia and trembled with excitement. There was a harsh clean love in Marcy. Her whole life was in this body—such peace.

Marcy changed into a sundress and wrapped her wet hair on her head with barrettes from Dalia. She and her mother were in the kitchen. Marcy imagined her mother at the stove stirring the butternut squash soup as she listened to Dalia's tales of crowded subways and markets. Her mother was laughing. Marcy didn't want her to stop.

In the living room the man sat beside the wood-burning stove. He looked up from his book.

"Marcy," he said, and smiled. "I want to talk about what happened. I need you to look at me when I'm talking to you." Her eyes met his. Hate was enthralling, desirable even. She sweated for it. "I'm sorry," the man said. "I shouldn't have said what I did." Marcy wanted him to say it again. She'd dare him to say it. "You and your mother have been through so much. I'd hate to add to it. I promise to give you your space."

Someone in the kitchen turned up the music. Dalia was singing along and Gloria shouted, "Who is this? I like this a lot."

Marcy thought she could be another woman in that kitchen. She could be enveloped in that warmth.

"I promise all of this on one condition," the man said. "There are so many books in this place, but I haven't found what I'm looking for. Your mother tells me there are more. Show me where they are?"

Marcy could have rushed into the kitchen and fumbled for her apron, apologizing over the music. She could have run upstairs and locked her bedroom door, but she was gripped by this man.

She led him to the supply closet where there were books and a light bulb attached to a string. She felt the man's breath on her neck as his hand flew up her dress. When his other hand covered her mouth, she bit him. He called her that word again. She ran before he could grab her. Dalia and Gloria were laughing in the kitchen as she rushed up the stairs.

She locked her door and pressed her back to the wall and sobbed until she was empty and still. Like an old friend, the music lingered at her door.

The wizard did to the second sister what he'd done to the first. But the third sister was very clever. The wizard gave her the same key and egg, yet when he left, she entered the forbidden chamber without the egg. She did not run when she saw the bodies cut to pieces. She did not scream. Instead, she gathered the parts of her two sisters and sewed them back together, and they rejoiced and held each other close.

On his return, the wizard saw that the egg was clean and knew the third sister had been true. She agreed to marry him on one condition. He must deliver a basket of gold to her father while she prepared for the wedding. Then she covered her sisters in gold and hid them in the basket and directed them to send for help once they were safely home. While the wizard was gone, the third sister found a skeleton in the forbidden chamber and dressed it as a bride and placed it in the window. Then she dove into a barrel of honey and rolled herself in the feathers from the wizard's bed until she looked like a magnificent golden bird. Soon, to her great surprise, she had become the beautiful bird. She circled above the wizard and sang into his ear. His bride, she said, was waiting in the window, the most beautiful bride in all the land. The wizard saw the skeleton and ran to her, but the sister locked the door behind him so he couldn't escape. Then her father and his kinsmen arrived to set fire to the house, and the wizard and his bride were destroyed.

By August, Marcy was spending as much time with Dalia as she could. The man had left the resort for another job, but Marcy was afraid he'd return. Alone, she imagined her insides folding into scarlet cranes wading in darkness. But with Dalia she opened.

They sat on Dalia's bed waiting for their toenail polish to dry. The window was open and the tree house cooled. Dalia's skin flushed with rose and gold. She wore denim shorts and a crocheted bikini top. Her toenails, like Marcy's, were light blue. She combed her hair before the mirror and talked to Marcy's reflection. "Some of my best childhood memories happened here," she said. "You're so lucky." Marcy shrugged. She wanted to smile but couldn't. Dalia's face softened. "I have something for you," Dalia said.

Marcy watched the fringes of Dalia's bikini hang in thick ropes between her legs as she opened a dresser drawer. When Dalia turned around, she wore a sequined mask in the shape of a butterfly.

"When I first moved to New York," she said, "I was scared and lonely. I started reading a lot about butterflies and made this mask. Sometimes I imagined myself becoming a butterfly. Crazy, right? Like, who am I to do that?"

Dalia's eyes were fierce behind the mask. When she spoke, the wings appeared to flutter.

"A butterfly emerges from its cocoon with its wings furled," she said. "It's very vulnerable. I imagine the butterfly all, 'Great, now I've got wings, but my home is destroyed and that cat over there might eat me. And now I'm somehow supposed to get to higher ground?'"

Marcy laughed.

Dalia set the mask in Marcy's lap. "It's your color. Keep it."

Dalia leaned back on the pillows and closed her eyes. Marcy tucked the mask into her pocket and crawled next to Dalia. She smelled like smoke, a spiced scent in the dark. This was closeness, Marcy thought. She stared at the blond hairs curled above Dalia's shorts. She reached inside and Dalia stirred.

"Marcy," she said. "Marcy, whoa."

Before Dalia could say more, Marcy rushed down the stairs and didn't stop until she reached the office. She wanted to tear the mask to pieces, but went inside. Light came from the kitchen. She followed its glow. Gloria sat in her bathrobe at the table. Her eyes were puffy. Her hand cupped the bottom of a near empty bottle of wine. Her other hand was balled against her mouth. Marcy watched the tears stream down her fist. Gloria wiped her eyes and drank from the bottle.

Marcy saw the heels of all the men who'd fled Gloria. She saw herself, for once, making it right for the woman whom right had barreled past.

"It's going to be okay," Marcy said.

"Only in Marcyland," Gloria said. "Only there."

In her room Marcy sat at her desk. She closed her eyes and saw young girls lured into the woods and hacked to pieces. She saw these girls putting themselves back together. They touched each other's bloody cheeks and an old courage rose in them. They transformed into birds, their wings made of gold. They circled their tormentors and gouged their eyes with their beaks. They soared and they sang.

Marcy wrote a letter to her mother. "Only in Marcyland do I wake up afraid," she said. "Only there am I afraid you won't believe me." Then she wrote about what that man had done to her, the last man that Gloria had loved.

She folded the letter in half and waited until sunrise, then slid the letter beneath her mother's door.

As she imagined Gloria reading the letter, Marcy put on the butterfly mask. She flew from her room and didn't stop until she reached the edge of the lake. The sun lit the hills.

The sky was a muscle of blue. Families camping across the water were starting to wake. Every summer Marcy had watched the love of strangers sluice through the trees like rain. She wanted to practice on someone, anyone, what those strangers knew. She wanted to know what it was like to be a beautiful golden bird.

"Marcy," her mother said.

Gloria had the letter. She was still in her nightgown covered with yellow roses. The wind whipped her hair across her face. She shook like nothing Marcy had ever seen. Her shaking was a wild song Marcy couldn't stand.

Marcy jumped into the water. When she rose, the mask clung dripping to her face. She swam on and on. Her legs screamed beneath the surface. When her body tired, she turned and saw Gloria on the shore, tiny, waving her arms.

"Don't make me come after you," Gloria shouted.

"You won't," Marcy said. "You *never* do."

Gloria swam as if her nightgown were weightless. The yellow roses flowed out in all directions. Marcy watched with a stinging awareness how her mother moved through the water. Marcy wanted to punish her. She wanted to sink to the bottom of the lake and never see the bloom of daylight again.

The mask had slipped from her face now and hung around her neck. Gloria didn't stop until she reached Marcy's side. Marcy turned toward her mother and cried.

"We're going to get him, Marcy. He won't get away."

Marcy's arms tightened around her mother, that billowing garden. Gloria pressed her forehead against Marcy's. When they pulled apart, the sun was high above. Marcy clung to her mother as they swam home. Marcy thanked her. Her mother told her not to. They swam on.

It's Either That, or You're Pregnant Again

A man gives a kidney because he doesn't believe
in God. Believe in Kickstarter, Facebook, Instagram,
in a copperhead coiled on the welcome mat.
There's a man dressed as Lincoln
in the delivery room. It's impossible
to know what the sniper needs,
but she's packing a sandwich anyway,
which is preferable, by far, to gnawing
at her nails. The differences between a baseball bat and gavel,
like the difference between justice and revenge—nothing
like the difference between revenge and retribution.
No, not anything we have to think about.
The remains arrive and are ready to be picked up, as is
the tab from the city, and the eyefuls of stardust
and ice, blue-gray like an X-ray or ultrasound.
Rah, rah, Rauschenberg, they cheered at the opening.
Pages of answers as from a deposition or teacher's guide,
utterly unreadable at bedtime.
The men from the forensic lab examine the prints
expecting to find the Minotaur, or (at least)
a complete man. My dearest, darling afterward,
how I've tired of your song.
Let my conscience be your guide, the iridescent
scales of it drifting into your orbit. The pen is the greatest
predictor of the future. Perhaps now's the time
I should forgive my father.
This afternoon I have a feeling that my windshield

will shatter, and—can you imagine—*me*, bejeweled
in safety glass! The red carpet. All a-glitter,
expecting an award. Open the aperture
and say "ahh." Eleven years old and it's serious,
look at her figure and ground compelling conviction,
her laying bare of the device! She's crowning.
And you will come to an opening,
when you come to an opening,
take a deep breath, blink, then fully open your eyes.

At Fenway Park

for Stephen Dobyns

Go, summertime. Worst one for me,
and maybe my punishment in Purgatory

would be so infernally hot
and coded with new money and ancient

histories of exploitation and control
that somehow sprout skyscrapers

like rabbits and deer heads raising
ears up in high grasses the colors

of their coats in the late afternoon light,
and I am pushing at the handles

of a desperate three-wheel tourist
rickshaw on wheels for the dock

with the last ocean liner in the world.
Ever notice how many people in the seats

around home plate at Fenway Park
in Boston smell beefy when they get

up to sing and stretch between late
innings, and the announcer does not

say that the following is a paid public
display of affection for kid soldiers

with taxi-door ears, and gobs
of tartar sauce on stretch pants

from all that fried seafood
and the ricotta-stuffed pastry

shaped like lobster claws. In some
other dimension, the faithful

tumble down empty dark tunnels
of poured concrete at game's end

holding giant half-empty plastic
cups of beer, and there are not

a lot of them, and certainly
they live in the enormous sheds

gathered around coal mines
and steel mills, pointing mouths

up to the heavens, not really
booing, but making a sound

that sounds like it, *whooooo-
ooooooooooooooooooooooo?*

Suicide Summer

The zeitgeist: lilac and blood orange.   The soundtrack: Flight
of the Bumblebee.   Summer of   too sweet then bitter. Torn paper
moons and little bits of grief.   Summer of triple-digit heat.
Men sweating in seersucker;   women at the mall,   not buying clothes
but looking at them, shopping for images—   something symbolic,
a discounted red scarf,   a gray bikini. It's summer   and everything
smells like gasoline.   Everything tastes like copper.   Sisyphus splits
from the office with a cardboard box of his stuff.   The guitarist
smokes Spirits backstage   and hums Summertime. Billie Holliday is
dead. Mick Jagger is   dwindling. Scentless death,   carbon monoxide
and lopsided skulls.   Summer of flypaper and malapropisms:
the crowd bursts into   applesauce.   God takes his suggestion box
and hides it.   Somebody's aunt is up on the roof,   she says she'll jump,
no one believes her.

The Most Beautiful Migraine in the World

The most beautiful migraine in the world
starts like small town fireworks
dome shaped and weeping
shoots of long burning silver
as I look across a darkening sky.

All the dogs start barking
to answer the bangs and reports,
the whistles and whumps that match
my tinnitus, my heart.

The whole world's abuzz. It glistens
like sunlight through a hat's woven brim,
with sprays of sparks, no tails
or trails, overtaking the small shadows
that normally cross my view.

After the small-scale pyrotechnics—
the Crossettes and Chrysanthemums,
the Roman Candles and Diadems—
the scattering of applause,
people head up from the beach.
Flashlights stutter along the path
to the cottage. Everything softens.
The last bottle rockets fizz and pop,
I close my eyes to the smoke and the stars.

Zane's Trace

POSEY

Yes, the school play. The difficulties. Cane or walker. The school is flat and walkable, which is different from the schools she suffered through until she was freed from that at sixteen. Father didn't believe in schooling, bunch a nonsense stuffed in. Get a job he said, so she did. But the play: her grandson Brady says it is about history and he will wear a top hat, so she will be going.

MISS ELISE

She wrote the play, but really it's the voices of the past that are important. She has no training, not really, just some poems she did in high school, when her English teacher was so encouraging, and yes, she took a screenwriting course in the teacher enrichment sessions at Wright State, but she's no writer, really. She hardly wanted to put her name on the playbill, but she did because it would look silly to have no name or to say "Anonymous" like those old poems in the literature book.

Zane's Trace, by Elise Southey. It looks very well, after all.

BRADY

The play is for school, but it will be fun. They have to know their lines by heart, which Brady can do because his mother helped him practice, and she made his brother help him practice, and he did it, although he'd rather play his new game. Brady likes that he will be wearing a top hat in one scene and a feather headdress in another. The play is about a road, but not a road like the one he lives on. An important road. A road through the forest.

POSEY

What to wear. Closet full of old lady things. She still has some stepping out clothes in the back, in a plastic zip-up. Those were the days when Kenneth was alive. A burgundy red dress with a ruffle at the sleeves, her fingers remember the feel of the weave. She wore it with a diamond necklace Kenneth bought her after one of his toots. A diamond no bigger than a sunflower seed but more than her sisters ever had. She'd wear it but the catch is too much for her fingers now, and Brady won't care what she wears anyway.

Her last grandson, for his mother has said she has closed the barn door and no mistake. Posey doesn't blame her. Brady's brother is a handful and Brady himself. There's no sweeter child but he has his cross to bear, as we all do.

BRADY

Today Brady does not want to get on the bus. He likes school but only when he gets there. The time of leaving and the time of the bus is like a torture, which he's not sure what it means exactly but knows is bad. He's in between, stretching out like Silly Putty, his mother standing in the driveway at one end and the school at the other, where he will have to use his sticks to help him walk. The bus smells and lurches, and he's not allowed to bring his Nintendo DS. The DS is not for school. When the bus stops, when he has gotten off, the slanting sickening feeling goes away. He gets his sticks under him and follows the others into the school. They have to be in a line. They mustn't run but they do, the others.

When Brady was smaller he had a walker like his mamaw's and then he could run but not now. The sticks are better though, his mother says. They are more grown-up.

MISS ELISE

"Quiet, children. Let's be calm." She says this a hundred times a day, but she doesn't mind. They are seven years old (some already turned eight) and they are full of life, which she honors. Strangely, although she herself is an anxious person, she is good at teaching. She likes everything about her job except those times when she has to talk to the principal, whom she finds intimidating, or parent meetings, when she always feels vaguely guilty and too young.

"Today is the play," she says. "Who is excited?" The children raise their hands and shout, which she allows for a minute before she shushes them. She ushers them to the gym, where they will have their in-school breakfast. She and Miss Michelle, who is Brady's and Caitlin's aide, walk along the children's straggling line, exchanging careful smiles.

POSEY

When you think about the past, although there is no point in that, but when you do. That long time ago in Tennessee, like another world, the dirt even a different color, red and rusty. When you washed it from your hands and your legs after they'd been out playing, the water ran red like blood. She and her sisters, in matching dresses, barefoot except for Sunday. None of the others wanted to know how to work the sawmill, but she said she would although her father said it wasn't for a woman to do. He had nobody else, couldn't make anything but daughters. He didn't blame their mother like some might have. Or not in their hearing. Was it always warm there? She thinks it was.

She hasn't been back since her mother died of cancer in nineteen and seventy-two, the funeral a three-day affair. Enough food to sink a battleship. All those still there, with their children and children's children, living their lives, but she and Kenneth had left that behind and now she was here without him, the bastard.

MISS ELISE

In the late morning, the children work on their spelling, and Elise sits at her desk dreaming history. Ebenezer Zane, road builder, war hero—she pictures him standing in a clearing on the edge of where the Ohio state line would be drawn, looking into the tall trees, his gaze like an arrow that would penetrate the impenetrable forest. She is a little in love with him. His vision of a trail that would cross Ohio, making a way that was better than the killer Ohio River with its floods and obstructions. The Trace went narrow through the trees, wide enough at first only for a man on horseback. The making of Ohio, if you looked at it that way. These children were here because of it, you might say.

Each child has two parts to play, one speaking alone and one in a group. She hopes that it will instill history into them. She loved history when she was young, and so why not these children, too?

BRADY

Brady writes his name at the top of his paper in big letters: Brady Darlington. He wishes his name was shorter. The spelling words for this week are all from the play. History. Trace. Forest. Pioneer. As he writes them down (three times each) he thinks about the play. He's not worried that he'll forget what to say. He doesn't worry, except sometimes if his mom is mad at him. If he breaks something or leaves his toys out in the yard. His mom likes to have things in the right place, which he has gotten used to although it makes no sense to him. Why isn't the yard the right place for his trike if that's where he rides it?

He likes to think, so he thinks about the play. He has four bits to say, two while he's wearing the top hat and two while he has the feather headdress. The past seems too full of things, if you ask him, but when he said that to Miss Southey last week, she looked sad.

POSEY

Lunch, a leftover potato mashed with some peas and Miracle Whip, a little ketchup for color, then wash the dishes, leave them in the drainer. When Kenneth was alive, he would sometimes dry, making a great production out of it, putting on one of her aprons and dancing around the kitchen flapping the dish towel. Fool man. Didn't know when to stop before she lost her temper, which had been hot then. They were the both of them easy to rile. Oh, the arguments they had, one or the other of them stomping off. Learned to drive so she could leave the house in style, didn't she.

A wonder that neither of the childer came out that way, as mild as milk, the girl and the boy both. Brady was a crier, which she didn't have patience for, but he'd grow out of it she supposed.

MISS ELISE

From the play:

> Ebenezer Zane: I will blaze a trail across the Northwest Territory.
> Member of Congress: What are your qualifications, sir?
> Ebenezer Zane: I fought in the Revolutionary War and defended Fort Henry against the Indians.

(Elise had dithered about using that term, but Ebenezer wouldn't have known what a Native American was after all. She was prepared to defend its historical accuracy.)

> Members of Congress as a group: What good is a road through the forest?
> Ebenezer Zane: It will improve trade and help make America a great nation.
> People in the crowd: We need this road!!
> Another Member of Congress: If you succeed, we will reward you with many acres of land.
> [Ebenezer Zane goes out (cross stage)]
> Ebenezer Zane: We must get our supplies, men. It will be a long trek to Kentucky.
> Jonathan Zane, Silas Zane (Ebenezer's brothers): We're ready to go.
> Tomepomehala (Shawnee guide): I will help you find the trails, chief.
> Betty Zane: I will go with you, brother.
> One of the men: It's too hard a trip for a woman.
> Betty Zane: I saved your bacon at Fort Henry!
> Ebenezer Zane: We will all go. [He stands and looks out over the audience.] We will need all our courage to find our way through.

Of course, Elise knew that Betty Zane hadn't gone with her brothers. But Elise felt the need of at least one strong female character, as an inspiration to her girl students. One of them played Betty as a woman, and one as a child, in a flashback; the other girls, perforce, were performing male roles or anonymous women in the crowd scenes. Betty Zane had had a baby out of wedlock before her first marriage, but this wasn't anything Elise thought her students needed to know.

BRADY

At lunch, he sits with Madison, who is his friend. All of the kids in the class are his friends but some more than others. He and Caitlin are the only two who have an aide, but he believes that Miss Michelle likes him better than she likes Caitlin because Caitlin is mean. Sometimes. She doesn't have sticks or even a walker. She has to sit in her wheelchair all day long.

"Do you know your speeches?" Madison has chocolate milk and pizza for lunch.

"Uh huh," Brady says, "but you know that part at the end where they're all standing around?" He wishes he had pizza, but his mother made his lunch today.

"It's when you're wearing the top hat."

"The hat keeps sliding off, and Dylan is going to laugh." Dylan is his brother.

"It's because you have to lean forward on your sticks." Madison pushes away her un-eaten pizza crust.

"I know but I think I cannot do the sticks?"

Madison looks at him, chewing on a carrot. "Without the sticks?"

"Or maybe just one. Like if it was a cane."

Madison nods. "Like in the history book." Some of the men in the pictures had canes. "Did you practice?"

"A little bit," Brady says.

It's not that he minds the sticks so much. He has his sticks and his walker, and a wheelchair, too, like Caitlin's, but only if there's going to be a really long walk. They are a part of his stuff, like his Nintendo DS and his tablet and his stuffed animals, and the toys he doesn't play with so much anymore, the familiar things that live in his room and that accompany him when he goes out. Some of them are important (the DS, the tablet, his monkey pillow) and some of them used to be important but aren't anymore.

The physical therapist had said to his mother that he'd probably always need the sticks, but maybe she's wrong. Maybe someday they will lie in his closet along with his Jake and the Neverland Pirate ship.

POSEY

When she went to Detroit, back in the '60s, she had been the strongest woman she knew. She could lift as much as many men and outwork all of them. She had gotten a job on the line assembling windshield wipers, and later moved to ignition interlock. Some women couldn't deal with working on the line, but she was used to men, how they spat and cursed and tried to get a feel of you. Working the sawmill with her father, he hadn't had the patience to look out for her. Learned to take it, didn't she. Learned to answer back smart and use her fists if she had to. On the line, she soon knew not to work too fast, how to fit in.

She met Kenneth there when he came down with a clipboard to inspect. Wore a shirt and tie, from the office. She sassed him back like she would anyone, but it turned out he liked that. Didn't mind a woman who was taller than him either. When they went to the courtroom to hitch up, she wore her sister's good dress, let down at the hem. They were both making good money then, before the car industry went south.

Brady looked more like him than her own son, around the eyes, and the way Brady's hair grew on the back of his head, how he held himself alert, no matter that he had those damn crutches to deal with.

MISS ELISE

Elise eats lunch in the office with the secretary and two of the aides. Chatter chatter chit chat. What the principal said yesterday, which kid bit someone on the playground. Friday night—one aide has a date, the other doesn't, says she's given up on men. They all laugh. Elise is not from here but from another small Ohio town, so she's only a little bit of an outsider. They kid her about things but not in a mean way.

Except the secretary. She doesn't like Elise, although Elise doesn't know why. The reasons she herself likes or doesn't like people aren't always logical after all. She thinks of it as if it were a math problem. The people she likes, those she doesn't, the ones who don't like her, the ones who do—occupying four quadrants of a circle. Maybe there should be a fifth though, for people who make fun of her, which brings her back to the play.

Why'd you want to do that, her brother had said when she was telling the family about writing it. Who cares about old Ebenezer Kane. Zane, she said, like Zanesville. Zany, her brother said, messing up her hair like he always does. She knows that the parents and families of the children will sit and look attentive during the play, but what will they be thinking, really? They wouldn't be there if their sons or daughters weren't in it.

The principal brought in donuts, the secretary says. Do you want one? Or are you dieting?

BRADY

On the playground, Brady shows Madison how he can walk without his sticks. He flings them up in the air and propels himself forward for a few steps, catching himself with the sticks before he falls. He can take as many as four steps this way. "I'm hotdogging," he yells.

Madison jumps up and down. "Go Brady, go Brady," she chants.

"You're going to fall and break your neck," Caitlin says, which makes Brady mad.

Caitlin is sitting in her wheelchair by the jungle gym. Neither she nor Brady can climb on it. There is a special swing for kids who are different, but neither of them use it. Brady can sit on a regular swing if his aide helps him now, and Caitlin just won't do it, not anymore. There is a zip line, which they can use if an aide boosts them up, but Caitlin won't do that either. The last time Brady did the zip line he fell off and hurt his foot, but he didn't tell anyone except for Madison.

He braces his sticks in the rubbery surface of the play area and takes off again, only two steps because his legs are tired by now. "I'm hotdogging," he yells, because he has to yell while he's doing it or it doesn't work.

POSEY

She was upset when they found out about Brady. Should've sued the hospital. The baby, curled up in his crib, beautiful—how could something be wrong. God doesn't give anyone what they can't stand, one of the church women said, you know we're all born to suffer in this world.

Posey felt it rise up in her, what she was as a young woman, when she fought anyone who tried to get one over on her, anyone who pushed her down, who so much as gave her a funny look. Imagined bracing herself on her walker and socking the mealymouth bitch right in the eye. God don't know what he's doing then, she said. He's got his head up his ass if that's how he does things. But Brady is strong and smart. He does good in school. He'd tried on his play hats for her, the top hat and the Indian one, happy as a bird. She won't stand for anyone's looks of pity. He is who he is, she guesses. Not a broken thing.

MISS ELISE

She supposes that she should identify with Betty Zane, but it's Ebenezer who speaks to her. When she was writing the play, she felt as if she could hear his voice saying the dialogue. A tenor voice with a little roughness to it. Ear-catching, if you can say that. It was an economic proposition, she knows, with the promise of land and increased trade, but she believes that Ebenezer Zane was in it for the adventure, that he was uplifted by the idea of the cleft wilderness. A man with a larger soul. He established a settlement that became a city, Wheeling—how many people can say that? Elise can't imagine founding a city, even with the help of three brothers, which Ebenezer had. Her own brothers would be useless in city building, she believes.

When the children practice their lines, she mouths along with them. She chose the boy to play Ebenezer on the basis of his height—Jimmy, he's the tallest in the class. Not the smartest though: he keeps forgetting his lines. Still, he'll look well onstage. The children are excited about the play, most of them. They like the idea of being up on the stage, except for Theresa, who is sick with anxiety. She has thrown up in the bathroom already and will again. And Caitlin refuses to say any lines at all, although she has agreed to wear a hat, straw with a red ribbon. She and Theresa will have the comfort of the chorus, though; they'll be fine. They'll all be fine. The play will go off, and the audience will be kind. All of Elise's wit and knowledge and, yes, love—all of it has gone into the play, and when it's over, then—well, she doesn't know what.

BRADY

After lunch is play practice. Brady has his two hats and he puts one on, then the other. He is the only one who has a top hat because Miss Elise couldn't find any more. When he wears the top hat, he is the mayor of the town and he says his speech:

> MAYOR: Mr. Zane, if you succeed, you will bring honor to our town. Don't fail us.

Brady likes the way "Don't fail us" sounds, and he says it in many unrelated contexts, like at breakfast. "Pass the syrup, Dylan, don't fail us." And when they are playing dodgeball at recess and his team is losing. When he wears the feathers he and the others say, "Who are you? Why are you crossing our land?" They point their bows and arrows at Jimmy Chase who is Ebenezer and are supposed to look mad like there might be a fight. But then everything is fine when Jimmy/Ebenezer tells them about the special road.

Brady never thought much about roads before, but he guesses they are important. He lives on a road and the school is on a road. The bus goes on the road from one to the other, and when they visit his grandmother in Cleveland they go on the freeway which is another word for road.

"What would we do if there were no roads?" Miss Elise had asked them last week. "If there were only trees?"

Brady can see this in his head, just trees everywhere, all green. You would go past one tree and there would be more of them, and then more after that. It would be nice—everywhere would be like the park. But it would be harder to walk. He's not sure he'd be able to hotdog it if there were only trees everywhere and no flat smooth ground.

POSEY

Her daughter says she will pick her up for the play, but Posey says someone from church offered. Someone did, but Posey declined. May be a cripple but can still drive her own car. It's sitting down, isn't it, just as she would in her own front room.

The play is at four, but she is ready early. Sitting in Kenneth's chair, she opens her handbag to check. Kleenex. Heart pills. Washed-out pickle jar of orange juice for the sugar. Card for Brady with five dollars. Lipstick. Coin purse. Roll of mints. Kenneth's wallet. Been there since that last time because his health insurance card was in it. She watches the wind blow the trees at the back of the garden. Bare this year and weedy. Only a couple of tomato plants in pots her daughter brought over. Can't grow a proper tomato in a pot.

On the dot of three, she hangs her purse on the walker and starts toward the door. Hump the walker up over the doorsill. Edge down the steps, hand on the rail, clutch and then slide. Pull the walker along. Step step over the grass. The walker catches on the crack in the driveway, dagnabbit. Click the trunk open and brace herself to lift the walker in. Easy as pie. Her shoulder gives a twang, but it always does. Along the car, step step, a twitch and a wiggle and she's in the driver's seat. Getting her legs in the last thing. There—seat belt and off we go, not even breathing hard or not so much.

This car is still Kenneth's car, bought in 2001 just before he retired. Gunmetal gray. She pats the seat. Yes, I'm sitting here, she says to him. Never liked to be her passenger but now. If he's haunting her, he can ride along and like it. Going to see Brady in a play, she says to Kenneth. He don't know what he's missing, damn him.

MISS ELISE

It's an hour before the play and the road isn't there, the rug that is supposed to be the road. She was promised that she could use the gray rubber backed rug that the janitor puts down at the entrance on rainy days, perfect for a road, from the audience you couldn't tell the difference. But now the secretary says the rug can't be used for this purpose. Elise is overcome, anger and fright warring in her, words rising up in her throat that she can't or doesn't say. She can't cry but she might. The secretary stands behind her desk, hands clasped, pretending to look sorry. Such a pity, she says. If only you had told me what you were planning. School property not to be used other than as designated.

Elise clenches her fists as if she would hit although she has never hit anyone in her life, or any thing. The play is ruined. To the secretary she says, "Well, thanks." Hating herself.

"I'm sure no one will notice," the secretary says. "It's the children who are the important thing."

Alone in her classroom, Elise cries a few tears, her face against the cool metal of the lockers. The children are the important thing, but the play that she made for them is important too, something the children can enter, can live in for an hour, can take with them into the rest of their lives, the bravery of Betty Zane, the resolution and inventiveness of Ebenezer, the faithfulness of his brothers and Indian guide. Native American guide.

BRADY

It's strange to go home and come back to school again in the same day. Hurry, his mother says. He has to wear a tie which is like Daddy's except that it's done up already. His white shirt was supposed to be clean but it isn't, and his mother is mad but not at Brady. He doesn't know who she's mad at. Dylan is complaining that he has to wear good clothes. Their cousin is coming with them to the play and their aunt. Miss Michelle's daughter Sierra is coming although she's in a different grade. His mamaw is coming. She told Brady that she'd be there with bells on. He knows this doesn't mean real bells.

Brady is on the floor by the couch with his DS, playing Super Mario Odyssey. He would like it if he could do this up until they leave and then in the car on the way, but he knows his mother is going to take it away. Stop playing that and be a person, she will say. He isn't a person when he's playing a game because he is inside the game. His fingers are the way to get into it.

When he started playing he had to get Dylan to read things to him, the things that Mario and Princess Peach and Bowser say, but now he can read them for himself. The little box of the game screen on his DS or his tablet is like a window he can see through where things happen. Mario runs and jumps when Brady makes him do it. He can't jump but Mario can. The play will be like that, he thinks. When they are on the stage it will be like in a game. They will all be different people. He will, and Madison, and Jimmy and Caitlin. Miss Elise will be the same person though because she is outside the play. Outside the game.

POSEY

Sitting in the car she takes time for a smoke. She hardly does nowadays, but she won't give it up all the way. Her daughter is always coming around with things she should do. Don't smoke. Watch your sugar. Don't eat the fat on the meat. No coffee after dinner. Seventy-eight years old and she can drink a cup of coffee at night if she wants to. If she wants to eat a doughnut, she gives herself a little extra insulin, fixes it right up.

All the time of Kenneth's failing she didn't smoke because of his oxygen. Maybe she resented that, but now she's put that time away as best she can. Kenneth thinning down, his big hands weak. His neck as scrawny as a chicken's.

She drags on her cigarette, holding it between two fingers like her daddy did, and watches people straggling into the school. New building, gray concrete against the green woods. The little school she went to was in an old church. Set in a field of tobacco, nearest tree a mile away. How hot it got in May. They had fans they kept in their desks, marked with a Bible verse.

At last she sees her daughter and son-in-law's car. The doors open, Dylan hopping out. Daughter opens the trunk. Son-in-law hands Brady his sticks and stands by while Brady puts one leg out, then the other. He leans forward on his sticks and stands up. Everything so hard for him. He lifts his sticks and his father jumps forward as if to catch him. Brady is laughing.

MISS ELISE

Elise has locked herself into the staff bathroom, too bad if anyone else has to go. It's quiet, pastel pink and green. The cool white of the sinks is a balm. She rinses her face with cold water, holds her wrists under the tap. When she was little her grandmother would pat her face with a damp handkerchief when she had a crying fit. Pat pat, the small skritch of her grandmother's embroidered initials, smelling of the inside of her purse, stale flowers and mint. Elise was the only girl in a family of boys and she treasured these moments of nurture.

She looks at her red face in the mirror. It's almost four o'clock. The children will be gathering in the little room next to the stage where the hat costumes are stored in a closet. She has not even changed into her good dress, but there is no road, and if there is no road, how can there be a play. Ruined ruined.

Her hands clenched on the sink, she thinks of Ebenezer. If he were a saint, she could pray to him, patron saint of roads, destroyer of the wilderness, bringer of the questionable boon of civilization. She imagines herself going out of the bathroom, out of the school, getting into her car and never coming back. Oh, if she could take Zane's Trace, finding it here and there on little country byways, barely big enough for one car, pointing her way farther and farther southwest.

BRADY

Don't fidget when you're up there, his mother says. Now let me fix your tie. She pulls it straight. She looks like she is mad, but she is only worried. Don't pick your nose on stage, Dylan says, and she gives him a smack. You'll be great, buddy, his father says. Dylan puts his backpack on for him and then lifts him up the three steps to the place at the back of the stage.

There is a little hallway that goes to the room where they're supposed to be and for a minute Brady is all by himself. Between his family and his class. He can hear the hum and bubble of people out in the audience. They are not supposed to look at the audience, Miss Elise says. Look at the other actors. They are actors when they are in the play.

This little minute of being alone is strange, no classmates or teacher, no mother or father, no Dylan. He lifts one stick and balances, puts it down, then lifts the other. Brady thinks about how he is inside the hall, inside the school, with the whole world outside, all the roads leading away from here. Behind him, he can hear feet on the steps, and he starts off, as if he had been moving right along, just like usual.

POSEY

She arranges her skirt over her legs, smoothing it down. Dylan is beside her, can't sit still for a minute. She gives him a mint from her purse, and he crunches it to powder before she can blink an eye. He wants to know if she's going to come to his band concert. I might could, she says. Dylan turns around in his seat to see who's behind them. His mother is giving him a look, but Posey doesn't say anything. Not her business to make him mind.

The curtain up on the stage shifts and wavers as someone bumps against it from the other side. Never did they act in a play when she was in school. Her father would have had something to say about that. Godless waste of time. Capering about like monkeys.

The program says *Zane's Trace, A Historical Play by Elise Southey*. Posey met her at the open house day. Short, with a little round head and a great bush of hair. Teachers should be teaching their business, her father would say, not coming up with made-up things, putting words in the childer's mouths. Why not though, Posey thinks. Dylan bounces beside her and she puts her hand on his leg to quiet him, his knee as firm and round as an apple under her hand. Her old hands. Bunch of bones, she thinks. Held together with spit and peanut butter.

MISS ELISE

Yah, Elise thinks, yah, you bitch, the language of the schoolyard coming back to her. She has defeated the secretary—she has got some duct tape and she and the janitor are laying it down on the stage in a double curve. Two lines of duct tape holding down a road of black plastic.

The garbage bags can be reused, she tells the janitor, and he nods. He has an unlit cigarette in his mouth, twitching at the corner as he works. "We've got this, no problem," he says.

When they tape down the last of it, Elise stands back. Better than the rugs, she thinks, a great arc, black and shiny. Not true to the pounded and cleared dirt of the Trace but more dramatic. Visible from the audience. "What do you think?" she asks the children.

They have their hat costumes on, coonskin caps and derbies, bonnets, feathered bands, the one top hat, all crowding and pushing each other, a collection of wild atoms, bumping elbows and knees. "It's the road?" Jimmy Chase asks.

"It's Zane's Trace," Elise says. "And you are the people of history, remember that." She takes Jimmy's hand and shakes it. "Hello, Ebenezer," she says, and he grins. She shakes the hand of every student, calling them by their parts while the janitor watches solemnly. Elise cannot stop smiling.

BRADY

Brady stands in the wings with Madison. The wings are not like on a bird, Miss Elise said, but Brady can't remember why. Madison is hopping up and down. Her two hats are a bonnet and the feathers. She and Brady will stand together to be Native Americans in the middle of the play. But first he's the mayor. He's also the mayor at the end, a different mayor in a different town but with the same top hat.

"Is Dylan here?" Madison asks.

Madison has a crush on Dylan, according to their mom. Brady heard her talking to Dad about it. "A cute little crush," she said. Brady doesn't mind though, he doesn't want the crush. Madison is his best friend forever.

Caitlin is sitting next to him, rolling her chair back and forth, almost rolling over Brady's foot each time. "Dylan has a girlfriend," she says, "if you don't know."

They both turn to stare at her. "What?" she says. "He likes that girl who lives on Goat Run/Honey Fork Road. My sister told me."

Madison tosses her head. "I don't even believe you."

Caitlin smooths her dress down over her skinny legs. "Whatever," she says. "He's in the fifth grade, which is middle school, if you don't know. You're like a baby to him."

"Don't be mean," Brady says, and then Miss Elise has put on the music that means it's the start of the play. He likes it. He thinks it's like the sound of the forest, crowded and grand, with a feel like marching. He pushes his sticks on the floor, feeling the rubber tips catch and hold. He can feel the people on the other side of the curtain, Dylan and Mamaw and Mom and Dad, everybody else's moms and dads and kids from the other grades. When the curtain opens, it won't be the cafeteria where they eat breakfast and lunch. There will be a dark space (Miss Elise had warned them) because the lights will be off except on the stage. They will be in the box of light for everyone to watch.

POSEY

When the curtains part she finds Brady by his top hat. He's standing on the left by a girl in a wheelchair. He's grinning out at the audience, his face a bright star. She hardly pays attention as one of the others starts to talk, keeping her eye on Brady. "There's your brother," she says to Dylan, and her daughter shushes her. Posey's eyes fill up, damn them. Just a bunch of kids, she hears her father saying. Kids doing some made-up stuff, better off if they did a job of work. She keeps her hand on the arm of her seat, holding to it, swallowing to loosen up her throat. They are so bright, the children, their faces are like stars, Brady's with the most shine. His blonde hair is like the sun. All their life ahead. It won't do, she thinks. Won't do. All going to the same end but don't think of that.

Dylan is kneeling up on his seat to see better while Posey sits stiff beside him, holding herself together. What's the use, she thinks. No use in this happiness, this brightness, when it all comes to the same, shriveling to a husk in a strange bed. No use, no use at all.

MISS ELISE

She hears the first words of the play which Jimmy has for a wonder remembered.

> EBENEZER [looking out toward the forest]: I have an idea for a road, all the way to Portsmouth.
> SILAS ZANE: Brother, the forest is too thick. How can we make our way through?
> EBENEZER: I know we can do it if we try.

Elise mouths the words along with them from the wings. She is aware of all the children standing in their places, moving when they are supposed to, as she had taught them. The stage lights shine down on them, reflecting from their glasses and their hair. Everything is right, the lights, the placement of the children, and the road, the road looks very well. An inspiration. "Go on," she whispers to Brady, the mayor, and to Madison and Caitlin, bonneted townspeople.

Out they go, Madison first, then Caitlin, the wheels of her chair with a little squeak, finally Brady, one stick forward then the other, moving downstage so that they can stand in the middle opposite Ebenezer/Jimmy and his Zane brothers. She can feel in her body all their movements. She's hardly surprised when Jimmy Chase forgets his lines as he starts off into the wilderness, but the girl playing Betty Zane whispers them to him, plainly audible to the audience. The two boys playing animals of the forest (a bear and a panther) get a little wild and almost knock over one of the cardboard trees. Theresa hides at the back so no one can see her, but she doesn't throw up.

When they are moving into the last part, Elise dares to look at the audience. The principal in the front row is impassive, but his wife is smiling. People are quiet, listening. They have laughed in the right places. Jimmy/Ebenezer has traversed the length of the duct-taped road and has arrived at the other side of the stage, at Maysville, Kentucky, where a delegation awaits him and his men. Elise allows herself to breathe.

BRADY

Madison has taken off her feathers and is wearing a bonnet with flowers on it. The ribbons hang down because she doesn't like the feel of them tied against her neck. Next to them, Caitlin sits in her wheelchair. Her hat is crooked, and Brady dares to push it with his finger to make it straight. Caitlin makes a face at him. In the backs of their heads are the speeches Ebenezer and his men are making as they take the last few steps on the road. The Trace.

ЕBENEZER: Here is the good city of Maysville. We're here.
ЕBENEZER'S BROTHERS, BETTY ZANE, AND TOMEPOMEHALA: We have made it. [Cheering.]

Brady balances himself. They're supposed to come right up to him because he is the mayor, but he wants to be the one who moves. He rocks back on his heels and raises his sticks. He can't shout because it's not in the play, but he whispers as hard as he can. "Hot-dogging it!" He takes one step and quick as he can another and he feels as happy as if he could fly. Someone in the audience says something but he can't hear. One more step onto the black plastic road. His sticks come down and he leans on the left one, the one toward the edge of the stage. He is the mayor of Maysville and he has a cane so he can stand up straight. He starts to say his speech but his left stick is sliding on the plastic just as if it was on ice and his knee starts to buckle.

Oh, Brady, Madison says behind him, and he is seeing ahead to how he will fall, how someone will have to help him up, how Dylan and everyone will see him on the floor, and Miss Elise will have her sad face.

But before that happens, Caitlin's wheelchair is right up next to him so that he can lean on it. She leans over to grab his stick which has fallen, and he is upright again. The top hat has come forward over his eyes, but only a little.

ЕBENEZER: Mr. Mayor?

Jimmy/Ebenezer is looking worried, and Brady wants to reassure him, both of him, Jimmy Chase who always looks lost in his head when they are doing math and also Ebenezer Zane, who has come such a long way along the road. The Trace.

MAYOR OF MAYSVILLE: The city of Maysville welcomes you. You must rest after your long journey.

Brady jerks his head to fix the top hat. Caitlin pinches his arm. "You are so stupid," she whispers fiercely in his ear.

POSEY

After the play there is a tea party at the back of the cafeteria, behind the rows of chairs. Posey sits at one of the lunch tables. Brady is sitting beside her. He has a bruise on his hand from when he almost fell, which he has shown her twice, but he hasn't cried. His mother had yelled at him and hugged him but now she's gone off to get some cups of punch. There's your teacher, Posey says to Brady. Introduce me now, like a gentleman, and he does.

"This is my mamaw," he says, and so she adds her name, holding out her hand like her father taught her.

"Posey Wray," she says.

"I hope you enjoyed the play," the teacher says.

Brady forgot to say her name, but Posey knows it, Elise Southey from over by Dayton.

"I almost fell," Brady says, "but I didn't."

"You never should of had that plastic up there," Posey says. "Too slippery."

"I know, oh, I know," the teacher says. "It was supposed to be one of the rugs but then the secretary—"

Talk talk talk, Posey thinks.

"Did you see me walk without my sticks?" Brady says. "I was hotdogging it."

"You were being a damn fool," Posey says. So like something Kenneth might have done. Never took a care of himself.

"You remembered all your lines," the teacher says. "That shows a good memory, Brady."

"I'm good at remembering things," he says, "but I can't remember a lot from when I was little. Before I was three. I was just in my body then."

The teacher is saying something but Posey stops listening. Just in his body. The place where you have no thoughts. It makes her think of Kenneth somewhere where he is the opposite, only his spirit, all thought, where he is his best self. Her body a place she might leave if she could. How you are before the long spate of thinking and doing, and then again after that is over.

MISS ELISE

She stands before the strange old woman. Her hair is combed and she is wearing lipstick, a slash of red on her wrinkled mouth, but she looks as if she might live in the woods, she has a wildness. Brady's grandmother is old. She is history herself, and Elise wants to ask about her life, what in her past made her wild and proud, what made her spine so straight. Elise feels judged, but no, she's not paying attention to Elise at all, really. She's looking at Brady as if she can see inside of him.

Brady is one of Elise's favorites, but what a strange thing he said. Unconsciously, Elise hugs her arms, holding herself safe from she doesn't know what. The play, now. The play is over, and it went well, except for those few things. Lines forgotten, an outbreak of gig-gling when one of the Zane brothers tripped over the bear, Brady's slip.

Should she speak to the principal about the secretary's unhelpful attitude? Safety of the students is paramount. But could she be blamed, or the janitor? Better to say nothing, she thinks. Everything is done and over. History made alive for these few moments. It's a small thing, but we are made up of small things, good deeds, memories, flashes of goodness, bright waves of hope. She says goodbye to Brady's grandmother, Mrs. Wray, who pays no attention. She is still looking at Brady, or maybe just past him. Everything should be the best it can be, Elise thinks. Nothing should be lost.

BRADY

The punch is red but it doesn't taste like anything. Madison sticks out her red tongue and they laugh. Dylan is talking to a girl and Brady wonders if this is his girlfriend. Except for Caitlin, all their class is sitting on the bleachers behind them, but he and Madison like sitting on the floor. He pushed his sticks under the bleachers and it is like he could be anyone down here. He shows Madison his bruise and the boy behind them, who was one of the Zane brothers, leans down to look. His mother waves to him, which means she wants to leave, but he pretends he doesn't see.

"Did you say thank you to Caitlin?" Madison asks.

Brady shakes his head, because he knows that Caitlin doesn't want him to, and if he does she would say something mean. The play is over and they are only their regular selves now.

He can see the cardboard trees on the stage from here. They look strange and awkward now, but he remembers that when they were in the play the trees were dark and mysterious, casting a shadow over the shining road. The Trace. Brady's mother is coming toward them, looking determined, and Brady pulls his sticks out from under the bleachers so he can start the long way to getting up by himself which he learned to do only this year.

Jimmy Chase stands up on the bleachers and calls out, "We will build a road through the wilderness," and they all laugh.

Brady stands up, balancing, and shouts with them all. "Don't fail us," he says.

Three Untitled Poems from the Manuscript "State of the Wards"

The dream was reserved for larger parties. It was reserved for parties prepared to embrace their station as filmed audience. The entertainment consists of arbitrary and unpredictable physical beatings, which still conform to recognizable rules of game play. Participation is both mandatory and unconscious. Something is decaying. You make a face. Whatever it is, its half-life is one twenty-fourth of a second. You're rapt, struck dumb with staring, knowing something is off. But you perceive no discontinuity in the action, which is frenzied and hilarious. You keep searching the room for something you're certain you've lost, under couches, in huge potted plants, behind hanged pictures. But you have it wrong. The card you don't know you're already carrying bears my name. Ask anyone.

You don't look like your picture. I didn't recognize you as you entered my field of vision, the way governments are not recognized. I was expecting someone more. Someone who seems. Please forgive me, my brief absence. Remind me what you were saying. My attention wandered when I noticed your imagination is almost perfectly smooth. They say a low drag coefficient will take you far in life. Remind me what I was saying. Was I asking for your hand figuratively? Or had I merely come to the conclusion that I required assistance in extricating myself from this rolled car? Either way, what's your answer?

An abrupt and merciless assault on the blood-brain barrier is how I start a promising Saturday evening. Passing right through the pleasure principle like a hot knife through glycerin. My eros and thanatos are in perfect equilibrium. My creatine levels were just now topped off by a professional, thanks for asking. Hypothetically speaking, I'm leaving you. I take no responsibility for anything I've done while not simultaneously narrating it out loud. I'm not naturally talkative; I just don't like the little silences you make. Lying presupposes more than I can claim at this juncture. We will make love. Then we will make too much of it.

The Dog

In the second week of her vacation, the general boredom Anna was experiencing had transformed itself into a kind of reckless impulsivity, and so the idea of a new face in the hotel bar was enough to compel her to sit there, on the patio that overlooked the pool and the bay, watching the new face eat. He was about her age, thirty-nine, and his dog, a well-trained German shorthair pointer, was sitting next to him, staring at his feet. The man was eating a plate of fish tacos and drinking sparkling water; she was drinking beer and, although she had already settled up her tab, she called the waiter over and started a new one.

"Another Peroni?" the waiter said.

He'd put a faint emphasis on the word *another,* but she didn't flinch.

"Yes," she said.

She still had two weeks left of her "retreat," and already she was dreading the inevitable comment that she would hear when she returned home: *Oh my god,* people would say, *it was so great of Ben to let you do that!*

Nobody would lead with *You look so tan!* Or, perhaps, *How did the writing go?* Or, even, the judgmental but well-intentioned, *You must have missed the kids so much,* nor the slightly worse, *The kids must have missed you so much.* No, everyone, and she meant *everyone,* would lead with praise for her husband, Ben. *Oh my god,* she could already hear her friend Flora saying, *Ben is a saint!*

The waiter returned with another beer. Anna's third. He had served her, over the course of the past seven days, approximately twenty-five beers, and he had judged her for each one.

"Shall I reopen the tab?" he said. She gave him a thumbs-up while she drank from the fresh bottle, then gestured for him to take the empty one away.

The man with the dog wore a blue watch cap and several days' worth of stubble on his face, as if he'd just come off of the docks in Maine. But they were not in Maine, they were in Clearwater Beach, and the only docks she knew of in the area were the small sponge docks run by the Greeks in Tarpon Springs. The wind was up and it was cool by the water—the locals called it cold—and she imagined that the hat felt amazing, a soft layer of warmth blocking the salty wind.

She found herself wanting his hat, to cover her face with it, breathe in the scent of his head, and then place it upon her own. And this is where her lust began.

He wore old jeans and a white v-neck, as if he'd been working at some sort of manual labor all day. She drank her beer and watched as the waiter brought him a side of grilled chicken, which he fed to the dog. The dog ate the chicken with a wiggled gratitude and then curled up again at the man's dirty Red Wing boots.

Had the dog not been so well-trained, so quiet and obedient and completely trusting of the man, she would not have spoken to the man at all—he was handsome in an almost dangerous way, the kind of man who could tell lies without consequence. But when she saw him again the next night at dinner (minus the hat now, as warmth had returned to the shore), she decided to say hello. He was sitting at a high-top table at the very edge of the patio. It was a Friday, nearing sunset, and the bar was crowded with locals just off work and tourists just arrived for the weekend.

"What an amazing dog," she said. "May I pet?"

"Of course," he said and smiled at her. She squatted down to pet the dog and felt the man's eyes on her breasts, which were not well covered by the sundress.

Even the most handsome of men, she thought, were helplessly predictable.

She noticed that the dog had on a harness that signaled him as a working dog. "Do not pet me," it said.

She stood up and apologized.

"It's okay. He's off duty."

"Well, thanks," she said. "I guess I'll try and find a table before the sunset rush."

She looked around the crowded patio of the bar, knowing there were no tables left and knowing her decision had just been made.

"You're welcome to join me," he said, and so she did, awkwardly shaking his hand as she sat down. She told him her name, Anna, and he told her his: Dmitri.

"Dmitri?" she said, completely surprised.

"Dmitri," he replied. "But my friends call me Tree."

"Greek?" she said.

"Yes," he said.

She nodded. "I thought so."

———

Over dinner they explained themselves as parents often do when traveling alone in beautiful places. It's as if, in order to build any sort of camaraderie, two parents must first convince each other that they know how undeserving they are of the solitude and paradise before them. She told her story first—the hotel and spa belonged to an old grad school friend, Teddy, who'd married into a wealthy family of hotel owners. Teddy, and his husband Mark, had insisted that Lila take some time to finish the novel she'd been writing since finishing graduate school ten years ago.

"Summer is a slow season," Mark had said.

"We will even cover all your meals and drinks," Teddy said.

"Oh my god," Lila said. "I could bring the kids. Maybe I could find a sitter a few hours a day."

"If you bring the children," Teddy said. "The deal is off."

"I'll have to talk to Ben," Lila said, and Mark and Teddy smiled and said, "We already did. He understands the urgency of your situation. He's giving you three weeks."

"Nice friends," Tree said, after she relayed the story. "Three weeks here? On the house?"

"I guess they thought I needed it," she said.

This amused Tree. "And what was the situation you mentioned?" he asked. "And, if you don't mind, I am particularly interested in the urgency of it."

She didn't want to explain how the winter had nearly killed her, how late January had found her walking into the freezing woods and wondering how many anxiety pills it would take for her to pass out and freeze to death without pain. The kids, six and eight, spent the whole day at school, and she used the time to go into the hopelessness and grief she was feeling. She'd set the timer on her phone each day for 2:30 p.m. and by 3:00 she would put her tears away and summon every drop of strength she could summon. By the time she saw their bus coming up the road each afternoon, she was shifting into her more familiar mode—*mom*—and found herself standing at the threshold and smiling. This was an act of Herculean will propelling her from dark to light all afternoon until she collapsed in bed at night and went back into herself and her gloom, which is what Ben called it, *your gloom*, though it was more than gloom.

"I was sick of my kids," she said, trying to laugh in a way that seemed spontaneous, as if the thought had just popped in her brain with jocular aplomb. "And my husband, if you want to know the truth—I was sick of him too."

The last sentence opened up like a window, and he went through it.

"Believe me," he said, holding out his left hand to show off his wedding ring. "You don't have to explain. Marriage is hard."

"Marriage is hard" was what people said when they were married and wanting to fuck other married people.

Next, they showed pictures of their kids to one another, sliding their phones toward one another, and that seemed to make the rest of the night okay. It was all on the table. The clarity of their love for their families. And under the table, she moved her hand to his leg.

There was something hot about the urgency of his response, and something sad about it too. She felt him thicken under the table and then he looked at his untouched steak and said, "I'll get the check."

He looked startled.

"We can give the steak to your dog," she said, and the dog thumped his tail.

In the morning, he was asleep in her bed and the dog was asleep on the rug at the foot of the bed. She left the bedroom and went into the other half of the suite, where the vast desk stood in front of the window, soaked in sunlight. All of her notes and her books spread out, the laptop still open from the last work session. She had intended only a short dinner break, but, obviously, she'd never come back to the desk.

She called down for room service and when the clerk asked how many people were dining she said, "Two," then quickly panicked. What if somehow Teddy and Mark noticed this on her bill? Would they judge her? She suspected that Teddy, at least, would be happy for her. He had no use for Ben after the affair.

Teddy would ask her, of course, how the sex had been. She hadn't had the chance to ask herself that—but, now that she was thinking of it, wow!

It had been good!

This seemed an unexpected narrative!

She'd found some satisfaction in it!

She wondered if good sex carried less guilt than bad sex. No, she didn't wonder that, not really. She was sure this was true.

The overflowing breakfast cart arrived, she signed for it, and then wheeled it next to the bed. She woke him up gently.

"You must think I am a terrible person," he said.

"No," she said. "What? You and I did something we probably shouldn't have done. But I don't regret it."

"How can you respect me after that?" he said.

"Why would I stop respecting you after that?" she said.

"It really is my first affair," he said.

"Mine too," she said. This was a lie, but her past affairs were not his business. "Why don't you eat something and then maybe I should get to work?"

"I feel sick," he said. His eyes shimmered with forming tears.

"Sick?" she said. "Like you're gonna puke?"

Anna hated puking—it was her Achilles' heel as a parent. When the kids had stomach bugs, she almost always had a small breakdown when it was all over.

"So guilty," he said. "I feel so guilty."

She went to the bathroom and brought him a Xanax. She popped one herself.

"This will help," she said. "Shut that shit down."

"What shit?"

"Guilt," she said.

Then she took off her robe and got back into bed and ate breakfast while he stared at the ceiling. He wasn't hungry, he said, apologetically, and gave the dog his eggs. When the dog was done, he stood up and she took him in. He had a short, compact frame, fairly well-muscled, and a hairy chest. He had a belly that seemed new. He seemed to be sucking it in. She had loved the feel of his ass in her hands. Ben had a flat ass, lacking muscle or even a hint of hair. It was the ass of a boy or an old man, neither of which was sexy.

"Would you like to stay a little longer," she said, and let the sheet fall from her breasts. Replaying the night before had turned her on again.

"I better let Tasha out," he said. He sounded spent and remorseful. "She had a lot of table scraps."

Hearing this Tasha stood and walked excitedly to the door. She was fond of them both, man and dog, and understood that Tree was wracked with guilt. The shake in his voice was one of disbelief and pain. She felt bad for him, remembering the thick nauseous guilt of one's first indiscretion.

"It gets easier," she said.

"Marriage?" he said.

She had meant cheating, but she decided to agree. "Yes, marriage gets easier. It just takes work. And forgiveness."

She didn't want to see him cry, but he was close to crying, and because of this, once he was dressed, and his attractiveness became overshadowed by his deepening guilt—"It was great, but I can't believe that happened," he kept saying— Anna was happy to see him go, and happy for the dog too, and she attacked the basket of pastries when they left.

But she was also happy when he rang her room at four o'clock and asked if she was ready for a beer. Men only felt guilt for an hour or two; after that, their lust would return stronger than ever. These were things she knew and knowing them, voicing them inside her own head, made her feel older than she was. She had just finished Skyping with the kids. They'd had a snow day; a freak May ice storm had hit the Twin Cities.

She shut her laptop and said yes.

"I can't believe this," Tree said. "I can't stop thinking of you."

"It's OK," she said. "Just come over."

Three days passed like that—she'd work all day, he'd call around four, they'd take a walk, have a drink, or two, or more, and then end up back in her bed at the hotel. They'd have sex several times each night and not fall asleep until well after midnight. She grew used to the smell of his sweat and slept with her face buried just under his arm, one hand fiddling with his chest hair. She slept well next to him, spent from their carnality, and he and the dog were always gone just after dawn, so they didn't interfere with her work. She didn't know where they went and on the third afternoon, when he arrived at the beach, she asked him.

It turned out that he was staying in town and not at the hotel as she had suspected.

"Tasha and I just walk down here for the sunsets, and to see some people," he said. He gestured to the beach as they walked along it.

"I don't think you're actually supposed to have this dog on the beach," she said.

"Tasha is a working dog. An emotional support animal," he said. "I train them for a living."

"So, wait. It's not your dog?"

"This one will be hard to give up," he said. "But no, technically, she's not. Tasha belongs to the organization I work for—but I've been such a mess lately, I've actually not worked with her the way I should be working with her."

"She's been emotionally supporting you?" she asked, meaning it as a joke, but he looked sober when he responded.

"Exactly," he said.

"What does she think of your affair?" she said.

He looked stricken when she said that. "Baby," she said to him, coming closer. "You need to forgive yourself. Adults do adult things sometime. Sometimes we are in survival mode. You're surviving."

He told her that perhaps his emotional wobbliness was related to the fact that he was cleaning out his dead father's home, which was up the road in Tarpon. He told her the plan had been that he'd go down for a week alone, get his father's things cleared out, get the pool up and running, and, in general, get the rather cluttered and unkempt place ready to sell. Then his wife and his kids would come down for spring break for one last Florida hurrah at Granddad's place. They would turn the house over to a realtor afterwards and hope the place sold quickly.

"It's paid off," he said, "so whatever we can get for it will be good."

"How's the market down here?" she asked, though she didn't care a bit about the market down here.

"Getting better," he said. "When we sell the house, my wife and I plan to pay off our debt and hire a lawyer and get divorced."

"Oh," she said.

His eyes misted again.

"Well, it's a common thing."

"Are you happily married?" he asked.

"We don't talk about divorce."

"Do you think about it?"

"Well, sure," she said. "Everyone does, sometimes."

"Do they?" he said. He was trying not to cry.

"If you're already planning on a divorce," she asked, "why do you feel so guilty?"

"I had been trying to save my marriage," he said.

"Maybe this will do it," she said. "Sometimes an affair can do that."

"I've never cheated on her in my life," he said.

She didn't have the energy to explain to him that she and Ben had an arrangement of sorts, something Ben had conjured up after he'd had an affair in Spain while she was stuck home with two toddlers. Back then, she had wanted to leave him but couldn't imagine how she'd cope with the financial burden or the public humiliation of being dumped by her husband of twelve years. He had wanted her to forgive him; he wanted to stay married.

Ben had suggested an open marriage in therapy.

"But I've used my free pass," he'd said, standing up and pacing about the room. "No lovers for me. But you can have affairs. You can take lovers whenever you want them. Just don't leave me."

"Lovers," she said. "Lovers is a ridiculous word."

Then he was sobbing in the therapist's office and she was afraid he might puke. She'd burst into laughter. "No lovers for you? Just for me?"

But he'd not seem any humor in this and nodded gravely, as if he'd just admitted to some act of heroism.

"That's really the arrangement you want?" she'd asked. "A one-sided open marriage?"

He'd insisted, through snot and tears, that, yes, it was.

"Okeedokee," she'd said to the therapist, who seemed to have gone silent out of shock. "I think our work is done here."

Since that day, he'd had, to her knowledge, no more affairs. And although she had no idea if he was serious about his proposal, she had, surprisingly, taken him up on his offer. She'd had six lovers since that day—their final session of therapy—and with each one, her revulsion with everything but the physical aspects of the male species grew deeper. She told Ben nothing of the affairs. Were they even affairs? Either he had been serious in the therapist's office or he had been manipulative. Either way, she was in the right. Don't say shit you don't mean, she used to tell her kids. You'll get hurt.

One of the things she'd learned about men: the maudlin, newly separated men, the men in marital hell, like Tree, were the most energetic lovers in bed, but the most emotionally exhausting people in the world outside the bedroom. It was a trade-off. For every climax, there'd be a long valley. But the climaxes were worth it.

"Let's drink," she said. "You seem to need one."

"I've been drinking too much," he said. They all said that, the broken ones, before they undressed you again. It gave them something to blame.

In his ear, she whispered something filthy, something she had said to men before in similar moments. It always worked. He grinned. All his gloom blew off towards the sea. They went to her room and ordered a bucket of Coronas. The beers arrived just after they'd fucked, hard, coming loud and unhinged. They both blushed as the room service man wheeled in his cart as they tied their hotel-issued robes.

"I've been standing out there for ten minutes," he said grinning. "You didn't hear me?"

"No," Anna said, smiling. "We didn't."

Her robe was half open. She looked over at Tree. He liked it. They'd each had one beer before he opened her robe again, began kissing down her belly. He was a better lover than any man she'd had before. As he went down on her, she ranked them as best she could, until she couldn't think straight anymore.

They spent one last night together, and in the morning, she felt her first pangs of guilt. Why? Who had she hurt? Tree dressed and left at dawn, and she refused him a tearful goodbye.

"You can remember me," she said, "but don't make me a part of your reality."

"What do you mean?" he said, as he knelt down to clip the leash to his dog.

"This wasn't your real life," she said. "It didn't count. That's the way you endure it."

"Endure what?"

"All of it. The infidelity? The missing me? You insist it wasn't real."

"You think I'll miss you?" he said, breaking up into teary woe again. "Because I won't."

He let out a snotty laugh.

"Every time you masturbate alone in your bathroom while your wife is asleep," she said. "You'll miss me."

She was stealing lines from her first extramarital lover, recycling the things he had told her. He was a Division II college basketball coach she'd met at O'Hare Airport during a blizzard, two weeks after Ben had confessed his own infidelity.

"Just be happy we had so many great orgasms," she said to Tree as he went to the door. "And if you want your marriage to work, Tree, I really hope it does."

"I love you," he said, and she nudged him out the door.

"I know," she said. "This is the moment when all men fall in love."

"Tonight," he said. "One last night."

"We'll see," she said. She gave the dog one last pet and then she shut the door.

The night before had a particular kind of urgency about it that had left the room a bit dank with the smell of sweat and salt. She'd not had housekeeping come in for the past few days—she didn't want to interrupt her work—but that morning she showered, dressed in running clothes, and called down to the desk to request a cleaning and fresh linens.

The beach was not crowded yet and although she had planned to run, she walked, feeling heavy. She was not, she realized, feeling guilty about the affair she was having—why call it anything else—but because she realized that she did not miss her life back home. She missed her kids, yes, sometimes very desperately and viscerally, but she didn't miss Ben with anything more than a faint fondness, and she didn't miss their home, or their own dog, a mutt much less well-behaved than Tasha, or any of the routines that accumulated each week to construct her life. She didn't miss her house, or her neighbors, or even any of her friends. She had no remorse over missing the baseball games and swim meets that were unfolding without her; she gave no fucks who'd won. The feeling thrilled her and terrified her.

Tree's family would arrive the next day—they were driving down from Michigan—and, if she chose to see him again, once more, it would, necessarily, be their last night together. Anna was relieved. She'd have one week for focused work—seriously, she would work eighteen hours a day and finish this book—before going home. She'd loved her time with Tree—the sex and the secrecy and the sweetness of it all had been just what the doctor ordered, if the doctor was a bit mad and had a belief in self-destructive cleanses—but she wanted to get back to work. She owed her kids that much. Besides, maybe she could sell the book if she'd finished it. She had a literary agent who'd taken her on a decade ago and was waiting for a novel to sell. And selling the book, even for a modest amount, might be enough to set her free. She would finish the book, sell the book, file for a divorce while publishing the book, and turn her life into one she would miss. Next time she traveled, she would have a life she missed, she would feel homesick, she would tell small crowds at bookstores about this trip, looking fetching in outfits she did not yet own.

She would become the kind of woman who said things like, "I miss sleeping in my own bed."

But she did not miss sleeping in her bed, not at all, and so when Tree called her that night, even though she was working, she dropped everything when he said that he and Tasha had pulled up to the hotel.

"Let's go somewhere else," he said. "Our last night."

They drove to his boyhood home after dark, pulling into the garage of the '70s-style ranch house.

"The neighbors all know me. They all know my wife," he explained. "We come down twice a year and stay here. I mean we did. My dad died suddenly. He was in good shape. Only sixty-four."

"I don't mind parking in the garage," he said.

They swam in the backyard pool with the lights off, completely naked. It had been years since she last skinny-dipped—that had happened at a party at a lake in Iowa years ago, in graduate school, when she and Ben were still in perfect shape and the thought of being nude in front of dozens of peers seemed somehow, if not appropriate, then at least acceptable.

She remembered Ben wanting to sneak off somewhere to fuck, but she resisted. She was having too much fun at the party, if she recalled correctly. Not a good sign, she thought—if you have a chance to sneak off and fuck someone on a beautiful summer night lit with fireflies and a waning moon and you don't want to do it, well—don't marry him!

She thought of this as she watched Tree press himself out of the pool, his thick shoulders flexing. He sat at the edge of the pool and she swam over to him, began kissing his thighs.

After he came, they dried off, dressed, and he showed her around the house.

"The Salvation Army was here today and took everything. We just have the beds left, really, for the visit, and the kitchen table. I saved some throw pillows we can sit on when we watch television."

"You want to watch television?" she said.

"I meant when my wife and kids arrive," he said. "Tomorrow."

He showed her his childhood bedroom, which contained a double bed, some taped-up boxes, and a suitcase. Tasha was asleep on the bed.

"I shouldn't let her up there," he said. "I'm doing a bad job with this one."

"The dog? She seems great. Or did you mean me?"

"I'm doing a bad job with you too," he said. "This should never have happened."

She put a finger to his lips.

"You wanna fuck me in your boyhood bedroom?" she said.

He recoiled. The fucker literally recoiled. The blow job she'd given him by the pool had made him come too hard and now he was still in that twitchy postcoital phase she hated in men.

"Why don't you just take me back to the hotel?" she said.

"Well," he said. "I do have a lot to do before the kids get here. And I should get to the store. Get some groceries. Laundry detergent. That sort of thing."

DEAN BAKOPOULOS | 53

"You'll want to wash your dick too," she said. "Scrub off my juices."

"Jesus, why do you have to be so fucking vulgar all the time?"

"What's your address?" she asked. "I'll just call an Uber."

If Ben ever caught her being unfaithful, she would always have the arrangement to fall back on as her defense. "In therapy," she'd say calmly, "this is exactly what you said I should do."

And he would have to admit what she always knew: "I didn't mean it," he'd say.

"You didn't think I would do it," she'd say back. "It was manipulative."

"Six lovers?" he'd say, in disbelief. The tears would come. Men and tears. Jesus, men. Stop crying when you're caught.

"Six lovers in three years?" she'd say. "That's not a lot for an open marriage."

And her deferred revenge would be complete. He could choose if he wanted to stay with her—a woman who took lovers on the side—or not.

Her first affair, the man at O'Hare, had happened because she was so angry. Her second affair, with a man ten years younger who worked in the supplement section at Whole Foods, she'd pursued simply because the sex of the first affair had been surprisingly good. The third affair was an ill-advised, whiskey-propelled one-nighter with an old college friend in town to give a poetry reading. The fourth man she'd met online on an app meant for singles and she'd fucked him in his car. The fifth affair had gone on too long, six weeks, and was with a stay-at-home dad who didn't want to have actual sexual intercourse with her; he often ejaculated on her feet while going down on her and somehow considered that less than cheating.

Tree was the sixth. Her favorite.

Back at the hotel, in her final week of the absurdly named "retreat," she missed him every day as she worked, felt his absence every sunset, and wished they'd parted on better terms. But she was a realist and knew the only way to work through any regrets and guilt was to finish the stupid book, so she worked almost around the clock, taking Adderall she'd bummed, a few months back, from a pepped-up woman in her book club.

Five days after she'd stormed off in an Uber, she finished a draft of the novel and it was shitty. She said it was done but it wasn't done. She only wanted it to be done. She posted on Facebook so her husband and friends could see a screenshot of the title page and the simple comment, "Finished!"

The next morning, she was eating breakfast at a strip mall diner a few blocks from the beach. She'd gone out for a run, but had ended up at the diner ordering steak and eggs and a short stack of chocolate chip pancakes. Her phone had died, and she looked around for something to read while she breakfasted. All she could find was a real estate magazine, so she flipped through the listings as she ate, and each house seemed laced with a potential new life that she wanted more than the one she was living.

When she paid her bill, she returned the real estate magazine to the small cardboard rack, and then she noticed and pocketed a stack of business cards for a real estate agent, Lila Burke. If you didn't scrutinize that tiny picture all that much, Lila Burke, it turned out, looked a little like her.

Later, she had the Uber driver drop her off a block away from the house. She was dressed in the closest thing she had to business attire—a black sundress and wedge sandals—and her dark curly hair was pulled back. She was wearing a pair of weak reading glasses from CVS, which she thought made her look a lot more like Ms. Burke's business card photo.

She rang the doorbell.

The woman who answered didn't look at all like Anna had imagined her to look. Anna had pictured someone short and cute, with a pixie haircut dyed blonde. But the woman was tall and lithe, darker than she imagined, and prettier too. In perfect shape, which was hard not to notice, given that she answered the door in a tiny bikini.

"Can I help you," she said.

Tree appeared behind her, wearing pajama pants and no shirt. She felt an ache flare up somewhere below her belly. Over the shoulders of Tree and his wife, she could see through the living room, to the lanai, to the pool, where children were hurling themselves into the water.

"Hi," Anna said. "My name is Lila Burke."

She handed each of them a business card. Tasha came prancing out of a back room happily, and Anna bent down to pet her. The dog was delighted to see her again.

"What do you want?" Tree said. He looked terrified.

"I'm usually not this forward," she said, "but I heard about your father. I live around the corner. He was a nice man."

"Thank you," Tree said. "But, we're not..."

"I was wondering," Anna said, "if you'd be willing to sell your house to me? As is. Save you the trouble of listing it. I own some rental properties in the area and I would, I mean, if that's what you want, I would love to buy it from you."

"Well," Tree said. "We're not sure if we want to sell it, exactly."

"What?" his wife said. His wife looked at Anna for a moment, then down at the dog, who was leaning against Anna's legs. "We do want to sell it, babe. The sooner the better."

That word stopped her. Babe? Was this a pet name used out of habit or actual endearment?

"Would you mind if I had a look around, and then I can make you an offer?" Anna said. "I'll be as fair as I can be."

"Well," Tree said, "it's kind of an intrusion."

But his wife waved that away, physically putting her hand on Tree's belly. "I'm sorry," she said to Anna. "This is hard for him. He grew up here."

She extended her hand. "I'm Leslie."

"Hi Leslie," Anna said. "You're so beautiful."

This made Leslie uneasy.

"Tree?" she said, "why don't you show her around? I'm gonna go check on the kids."

"Actually," Tree said, "they wanted me to come play with them. I was just about to head outside. Can you do it?"

The tension between them was a hateful one. Anna now knew the marriage she had come to observe was dying. Tree had been telling the truth. The terms of endearment and gestures of affection were meaningless—sad, old habits.

They walked through the house, which Anna had seen, but which she pretended to be seeing for the first time. Leslie stayed in the bikini, full and spilling out of the top, the bottoms creeping up her amazing ass. She was taller than Tree. The dog stayed at Anna's side, tail wagging, looking for more pets.

"He likes you," Leslie said.

"What a well-trained dog," Anna said.

"That's what my husband does for a living," Leslie said. "Trains working dogs."

Anna told her that was fascinating.

When the tour was done, Anna said, "I mean, you have a very nice family here. Maybe you want to move to Florida yourself someday? Tree's father used to talk about you all, fondly."

"You knew Daniel?" Leslie said.

"A little. He sometimes sat out in the driveway at night and I would walk by with my dog. He was a chatter. I think he was lonely."

"That's so funny," Leslie said. "You could barely get him to say two sentences on the phone. I always thought he was a quiet man."

"In his own way," Anna said. "Maybe after he had a few beers in him. Sometimes he stopped and we'd have beers. Near the end."

"Whoa," Leslie said.

"What?"

"We didn't know he was drinking again?" Leslie said. "But that might explain the suddenness of the heart attack. He wasn't supposed to drink."

"I'm sorry. I'm intruding. You're obviously not ready to sell," Anna said.

"Oh, no, we are," Leslie said. Then she lowered her voice. She touched Anna's elbow and leaned in. Anna looked down at her cleavage then into her green eyes. "We're going through a divorce, Tree and I. We never told his father. We haven't told the kids yet either. But a quick sale would be a godsend."

"Would it?" Anna said. "Oh, I'm glad. I thought maybe I had overstepped my boundaries here."

Leslie's eyes were drowning then and Anna reached over and touched her shoulder awkwardly. Soon, they were hugging and Leslie was really crying.

"I'm sorry," Anna said. "This is a terrible part of my job. Buying houses when a family is still grieving. I should go. It's too soon."

"Nonsense," Leslie said. They both looked out the window at Tree swimming with two boys, both of them around the age of ten, Anna guessed.

"I'm a mess," Leslie said. "I'm so sorry."

Anna looked at the kids and gestured out the window.

"Twins?" Anna said.

Leslie nodded. "I've been a stay-at-home mom for a decade. I'm exhausted."

"Well, look," Anna said. "Let me let you get back to family time."

"He's a cheater," Leslie said. "That's why—I can tell you're wondering why would a nice family like this fall apart. Well? Well, he's a cheater. He's had seven affairs that I know about—seven!—and I am sure there's more. I know there's more."

"I'm sorry," Anna said, trying not to flinch.

"It's ridiculous how much I still love him," Leslie said. "I still let him fuck me. Why? Why would I do that?"

"I'm sure this is hard," Anna said. "I shouldn't have come here."

Leslie stood up straight, her posture going from slump-shouldered sobbing to tall, together. A model's gait returned and she smiled. "You're sweet," she said.

"No," Anna said. "I'm not."

"Look, we're very interested in selling," Leslie said. "I'll have Tree call you, tomorrow? He'll handle this. I'm sure we can work out a price. I'll talk with him tonight. I think he's having trouble saying goodbye?"

"It's a lovely house," Anna said. "It'd be hard to say goodbye."

Leslie laughed. "I mean to me! But yes, to the house too!"

"He wants you to forgive him?" Anna said.

"He swears he's changed," Leslie said. "How do you know though? How can you tell with men?"

"With anyone, really," Anna said.

Anna took her last business card from the pocket of her sundress and asked for a pen.

She watched Leslie prance about looking for one, and then she wrote down her own cell number on the card.

"That's my personal cell phone," Anna said. "Have Tree call me there, would you? Whenever he's ready, I'd like to talk with him."

"Of course," Leslie said and walked her to the door.

Before she left, Anna squatted down and let the dog lick her face as she scratched his head. "I hope I see you again," she said to the dog, but not to Leslie, and then she left, walking several blocks before taking out her phone and sending out a signal into the world, a ping a working stranger would see and know she needed a ride.

White Oak Shadow Half a Mile Away

for Charles Wright

One thing I hadn't noticed before
is a tree that's standing on a hill
nearby, and I had to climb a hill
that's nearer in order to see it. Declining
November light, a solitary
tree, and its shadow darkening
the hill behind it like a smudge
of India ink. And I saw the shadow
before I determined the tree was there,
a dreamy little paradox.
To determine means you reach the end
of something, but I don't think I've reached
the end of the tree. It's entered my mind
and I'll keep looking at it there—
a thought or two will come from it,
I suppose. The tree will leave a mark.
I'm fine with that. It's good to have
a tree alive on a hill in your mind,
and then to study the actual tree
to see if it has other aspects.
The tree must be an oak because
the leaves are still attending it
like a bunch of people who haven't been
let out of church. That ought to evoke
a Scripture or bring to mind a hymn,
but I can only summon the story
of Zacchaeus, who climbed a sycamore,

and I don't think that really applies.
But that's all right. It's nice to have
something to think about and not
know where you're going. You'll come back
to it some day and then you'll know.
You have to believe that things come back,
though when they do they may have changed.
I don't know why I said the shadow
looked like a smudge of India ink—
it's not like I have a special thing
for India ink. It's just an expression,
it's just something that came into my mind
and it seemed like the right thing to say,
because the shadow looked like a smudge
of something that from a distance was dark,
that was made, ironically, by the light.

Frogeyes

An old man told me once
if you shake a jar of moonshine
and two bubbles roll together
at the brim of the jar, it proves what's in
the bright realm below is the kind
of shine you'll want to drink in small,
judicious sips. He called the bubbles
that roll together frogeyes,
and shook the jar he had to show me.
It's a very accurate description,
yet there's something upside down in
the image, which is the rest of the frog,
stuck to a heaven out of view.

I noticed once peering down from
a branch a pair of raindrops
and even saw reflected in them
upside down the little blur
of the world they captured—black branches
and the blank, silent speck of distance
reaching back beyond the blur.
Two tiny drops to see
and see inside, yet tinier
in each, a world turned upside down
and the scarecrow figure that was me,
and green-gray peeping frogs,
not birds, were singing from the tree.

Self-Portrait as Disco Ball Missing Tiles

the first mirror was a bowl of dark water / was a bowl

of dark water / & here I am

to make your party   imperfect / the first mirror was / today,

I am / why don't you check your reflection

inside of me / nobody wants to see their own face

to the nth power / I am trying   to laminate my brain / install

me in the cab of a tractor / install me   in a river so that

I may sun / install me   over this grave / could you put me on top

of a sick tree / install me on a clothesline / the first mirror

was a dark bowl of water / was a mirror / a bowl of dark

the first / could   I / could I just

warp your image

Morning Morning

Being a carpenter's dxxghtxr
I am afraid of power tools
& tormented by bad wiring
and being a carpenter's dxxghtxr
there is at least one
empty secret compartment
in the room If someone
else builds your secret compartment
it isn't a secret I've seen
an apple cut open That's how I know
they're all full of stars
My closet is full of invisible underwear
invisible coats
                invisible boots
I strategically
place the philodendron to cover
my chest & the aloe plant
to cover I am hoping to see you
again I won't ask that question
I am wearing blue garden
gloves This way I don't have to feel
the surfaces of things My father
doesn't trust me I can't blame him
I tried to weld I was so in awe
of the arc I burned through the electrode
without touching the metal

The Light in the Woods

He packed the camping gear into the trunk of the Nissan. His wife, Jackie, came out of the open garage onto the driveway, barefoot, wearing paint-stained jeans.

"Go ahead, run away," she yelled, although she was just a few feet away.

Saunders didn't look at her. "We've talked about it. We don't have enough saved."

"I don't want to teach history the rest of my life."

"We can't afford it," he said.

She went closer to him. "You don't think I have talent." Her foghorn voice carried.

Saunders looked around to see if any neighbors were out in their yards, enjoying the show.

He closed the trunk, trying not to go over the past. They had moved to this neighborhood because she had insisted, and it had gone to the dogs. And he had never liked the house, but they bought it because she loved it, and it had been nothing but problems. Cracked foundation, rotting window frames, piles of money.

In their years of arguments, ending the marriage had never been mentioned, but their daughter Emily was an adult and on her own now.

Jackie ran into the house and brought out her most recent painting, an abstract of primary colors on black. She held a paring knife in her hand. "Here. I know this is how much you value my work." She slashed the canvas and threw it at his feet, then pulled her long grey hair back with both hands.

Saunders turned his back on her, hunched his lanky frame behind the wheel of the Nissan, and drove off.

He cursed when he saw three other cars in the parking area of the state park. He wanted complete solitude, didn't want to even see anyone.

He hoisted the gear onto his bony back and hiked into dense forest, off the trail. Saunders had known these woods forty years, since high school. If he could glimpse the highest peak of the Catskills between the treetops, he would not get lost.

A clearing in the woods was too inviting to pass up, the ground covered with crimson and ochre leaves. He put the tent and backpack down. The dappled shade from the trees, coaxed into a dance by the breeze, turned the dazzling leaves into a kaleidoscope.

After he set up his tent, he opened the folding chair and tried to read, but the silence soon gave way to the seductive chuckle of running water. He followed the sound and found a small, clear stream, the smooth pebbles on the bottom looking like a tufted cushion. It was warm for October, and he stripped off his sweaty clothes and waded in.

Sitting on the rocky bottom, he saw his penis and scrotum distorted, the image undulating under the clear, flowing water. He had always been fascinated by the properties of light and its distortion, the basis of optometry, his profession. But what his genitals looked like now, in or out of the water, was irrelevant. Sex and procreation were things of the past, and had resulted only in fleeting pleasures and in Emily, his only offspring, almost as ill-tempered as Jackie. He wished his testicles had produced a more sedate person, maybe the son he had always wanted.

Or had they? An episode from his days in college came to mind. Rafaela, a student with whom he had a brief affair, had left school abruptly a few months later. The following year, a mutual friend told him Rafaela had committed suicide soon after the birth of a boy. Saunders knew the timing of the birth was consistent with his being the father, and a certainty if she had been monogamous. The boy was being raised by the grandparents, the gossip said, in upstate New York, not far from the college. Saunders had already been engaged to Jackie by then, and was too afraid of her wrath to track down the boy's Italian grandparents. "So who knows," he said to his testicles now, "Emily might not be your only creation. I'll bet you're relieved."

Back in his camp, he saw that his stacked provisions had been moved. He suspected raccoons, although as nocturnal creatures they only came out in daylight when sick. The container that had held the meat loaf was empty and on the ground. He knew the smell might attract more critters, and he took it down to the creek to rinse it. A crow sipping at the edge of the stream, where he had bathed, gave him a quick look and flew off, the iridescent feathers flashing like mini-rainbows.

He wasn't sure he was seeing correctly as he returned to camp. A man dressed in a brown uniform was going through his supplies of food.

"Excuse me," Saunders called out as he entered the clearing. "What do you think you're doing?" The man spun to face him and drew a knife from his pants pocket. Saunders froze, and the stranger approached him. He considered running off, but he didn't want to risk being caught by this much younger, muscular man.

"I'll cut your head off if you don't do as I say." He was around thirty, swarthy, and his black hair was cropped short. The knife in his hand was huge, a ten-inch chef's tool. "Lie down face up."

The man tied his ankles and wrists together with a length of green nylon rope Saunders had left by the tent. When Saunders stood up, he could only take small steps, and his hands could reach only to his chest. The stranger went through Saunders' pockets until he found his cell phone, smashed it on a rock, and pocketed the money in the wallet. He sat in the chair with a container of tuna salad, and when he was done he tossed it into the woods.

"The smell might attract raccoons. They can carry rabies."

"Shut up. Don't talk unless I ask you something." The man had dirt on his cheeks and ears, and a thick stubble of black beard. He sat and stared into the woods as the gloam deepened. He jerked his head in one direction or another every few seconds, as if startled, and walked out into the trees, arms gesturing. "Don't talk to me now!" he yelled at the treetops. His eyes were sparks of amber in the dimming light.

"I haven't said anything," Saunders mumbled.

"Not you! Just shut the fuck up."

The man held his head in his hands and rubbed his temples. "Stop!" he cried out, and dropped his chin.

The man was weeping, and Saunders knew he was witnessing a psychotic hallucination. Years ago he had heard from his mother that his uncle suffered from them, and had broken her arm during a particularly violent episode.

Eventually the man went to the tent, took out the sleeping bag, and laid it out on the ground. "Go in the tent," he said, his voice a hoarse whisper. "I'll sleep just outside the flap. If you try to come out, I'll kill you."

Saunders' ankles were tied so close that he had difficulty crawling in. He watched as the opening was zippered closed from the outside, and was able to sleep only in spurts on the hard ground.

When he saw sunlight through the yellow nylon of the tent he heard the man get up. He could hear the man's urinary stream on dry leaves, and then the door flap opened.

"Get out."

Saunders crawled out of the tent, his thighs shaking with fear.

The intruder got two apples from a plastic container, gave one to Saunders, and munched on the other. Saunders ate with difficulty because of his restrained hands and did so without much appetite. He was relieved that this man at least had given him an apple, and he took it as a sign that the stranger was not necessarily intent on hurting him.

The man seemed to go into a trance after he ate.

"Is there something I can do to help you?" Saunders asked.

The stranger seemed to be caught off guard, and he frowned. "Like what?"

"I have a car. I can drive you wherever you need to go."

"Not today. They'll be looking for me on the roads."

Saunders waited, wondering what else he might say to put this man at ease. He felt his mouth dry as dust, his saliva gone.

"Where will they take you if they find you?"

The piercing yellow eyes were like a feline predator's. "Back to the hospital."

"Not a prison?"

The man laughed. "Worse. In prison at least I'd have a chance for parole. Not at Green Mountain Psych. I'm there for life."

"They probably won't be looking in this area. I didn't see any cops on the way here yesterday."

"Maybe tomorrow."

The stranger frowned at the bushes, and Saunders moved away and sat on the ground against a tree. His arms were stiff and his wrists were chafing. He could feel his bladder, full from the overnight, sending him urgent signals. The rising sun was beginning to show above the foliage. "My bladder is full," he said. "I have to relieve myself."

"Go to the edge of the clearing, where I can keep an eye on you."

Saunders went a few feet, facing away from the man, and tried to undo his pants. "I can't open the zipper," he said over his shoulder as his bladder reached a crisis point.

The man went to Saunders and unzipped his pants. "You're on your own now."

Saunders moaned in distress as his tied hands struggled without success to find his penis through the underwear. The stranger watched for a few seconds before undoing Saunders' pants and pulling everything down, then stepped behind him. When Saunders was done and had pulled his pants up, the man zipped up the fly and tied his belt.

"You're a real wimp," the intruder said when they had returned to their spots.

"I just couldn't open the fly with my hands tied. I'm sorry."

"That's not what I mean. You didn't tense up when I tied you up yesterday. You haven't asked me to loosen the rope, not even to take a leak. Instead you wanted me to help you. And now you want to drive me to get away?" The stranger chuckled, but then his eyes squinted at Saunders' face. "Stockholm syndrome."

Saunders frowned and gave his head a little shake. "I don't want to join you. I want to help you get away so that I can be left alone."

"Getting away is exactly my goal. But I can see you like to obey me. And the way you make eye contact with me. Like you're trying to connect or something. It's Stockholm lite."

"I just don't want you to hurt me."

"You won't get hurt if you do as I say. And what's the big deal about being alone? You must be a loser, here by yourself, and you probably have a shitty job."

Saunders hesitated, then said, "I'm an optometrist, actually, and I have my own business."

"Oh yeah?" His voice was mocking. "I'll bet it's a crappy little place. And you probably let someone else run it."

Saunders said nothing, remembering that in fact he delegated the running of the practice to his manager.

"And I don't even have to ask who wears the pants at home, if you're even married."

Saunders blushed. He had gone from his parents' house to the college dorm, and then had married Jackie before graduation.

"Cat got your tongue?" the man jeered. "I've met people like you before. I'll bet you've never called the shots, not without—" He stopped suddenly and looked into the woods.

Saunders heard it then: an unmistakable crunching of leaves underfoot, coming closer. It sounded like more than one person.

The stranger took the knife out from under his belt, pulled Saunders out of the clearing and behind some tall shrubs. Saunders felt the edge of the knife against his throat. "If you make a sound, you're dead," the man whispered.

There were men's voices coming from the clearing, and Saunders could hear one of them say that the tent was empty. The intruder pressed the edge of the knife hard against the skin of Saunders' throat with a shaking hand, and he felt the sting of a cut as the man began hyperventilating. He could smell the man's stale breath mingled with the stench from his body.

The sound of rustling leaves came closer. They were going to be found, and Saunders thought his throat, which was already oozing blood down to his collar, would be slashed. Suddenly the man released him and ran into the woods.

The men, hearing leaves being trampled, rushed around the shrubs and into view. New York State Troopers. Saunders almost collapsed with relief. "Over there," he said, waving his tied arms in the direction the man had run. One of the officers stayed behind and cut the green nylon rope while the other two sprinted into the woods after the runaway.

Jackie looked more puzzled than surprised when Saunders returned home ahead of schedule with a half-inch cut on his neck. When she asked, he gave her a sketchy account.

"It just looks like you cut yourself shaving. Anyway, you don't seem very upset about it."

"He just tied me up. Didn't really mean to hurt me, I don't think." He walked out of the kitchen and into the bathroom to clean the wound. "It was all okay. He fed me an apple."

The local newspaper carried the story in two short paragraphs at the bottom of the front page. A reporter somehow found Saunders' telephone number and called, but he declined to be interviewed. He wanted to keep the experience private for his own sake, not only Ralph's, which was the man's name, according to the paper. The brief article also reported that years ago Ralph had killed his wife with a knife during a psychotic episode.

The following week he phoned Green Mountain Psychiatric Center and asked about visiting hours. The security guard on the phone asked his relationship to Ralph, and he said "uncle." After he was escorted through a number of locked metal doors, Saunders was brought into a room with green walls and four metal chairs. Ralph was brought in by a large man in a blue uniform, wearing a gun in a holster. The guard made Ralph sit down.

Ralph looked neat, clean-shaven, and his eyes were a dull brown. The fierce, yellow light Saunders had seen in the woods was gone. "Why are you here?" Ralph asked in a monotone.

"I wanted to see how you were."

Ralph looked at him, his face a death mask. "I'm fine."

He had not told Jackie where he was going, just out for a drive to think, he had said. Yesterday, after another argument about her retirement, she had offered to separate, maybe divorce, and he had declined without hesitation, a knee-jerk response. Now he was missing the menacing, controlling Ralph, and he understood, looking at this pacific, medicated version, why he hadn't taken Jackie up on her offer. He would have to spend the rest of his life with her, because an independent life was too much responsibility. And it was too late to find someone else to blame for his failures and disappointments—a hostile daughter, a faltering business—and those he was sure to garner before he died.

"They have my contact information here. If there's anything you need," Saunders said.

Ralph looked at him, blank, and looked down at his thighs.

They remained silent, Ralph with his eyes down. The guard was starting to look annoyed and grumbled something unintelligible, and Ralph stood up and walked out of the room, the guard behind him.

The optometry practice struggled on for many years until Saunders closed it when he turned sixty-eight, tired of working and unable to find a buyer. Jackie's paintings sold modestly, barely covering the cost of the art supplies, and they remained married in a dull truce and modest retirement. Saunders visited Ralph three or four times a year. They were brief and mostly silent visits that brought Saunders an edgy comfort.

When Ralph turned fifty-five and, under better medication, had been out of the institution fifteen years, he went to Saunders' funeral the year after Jackie's suicide. Through those years, the two men visited the clearing where they had met several times, and ate sandwiches by the stream. Those times together were mostly silent, except for the knowing cluck of the running water. After Saunders' funeral, everyone attending the burial gathered at Emily's house. She gave Ralph a canvas bag. "He wanted you to have this," she said, handing it over without making eye contact. She had been indifferent to Ralph the one time they had met.

When he got home and looked in the sack, Ralph found the green nylon rope he had used to tie up Saunders. The frayed strands from the two cut ends had been woven together into what's known as a blood knot, famed for its complexity and its strength.

Counterpoint: Twenty Years

We drove three hours north to see *All the Nations Airports*.
    We drove six of sixteen hours south to find ourselves
    high-five distance from the grill of the semi dancing
We never turned the music off once. We gave every song
    us down the highway. I said to it, *stop hitting me*. I said,
    don't flip us. We slid to a stop on southbound 95. Gave
every bit of breath we could force out in something like a tune.
In the club, the first notes of *Strangled by the Stereo Wire* set
    a second to fate. We stumbled up to the guardrail, the cat
    in hand, the car stuck to the truck. No one bleeding. Then
the crowd a-whirling. The bass, thick. The drums kickin' and Eric
leaning his full height into the microphone like he could push
    the onlookers began making calls. The EMTs asked after
the air any harder. The guitars screeched the walls into bat noise,
    our states of mind, examined us quickly, had us sign off.
into slim pitch and stutter. Slammed us into the night like we asked
    They said the car was drivable. The cops cleared us. We left.
them to. The second verse shook the windows, this pilgrimage.
    It was all so matter of fact, not dying, so gloriously quiet.

Tool Box

When he gave me the one his father had
given him, he said, "A good tool invites you
to pick it up." His were hands that held many.
Knew the difference between the weight
and balance of a ratcheting wrench
and a spark plug wrench. His were arms
that lugged power tools, hand tools,
vintage woodworking tools, garden tools,
and a lunch pail of the kind
no one owns anymore. His was
a back bent beneath the labor only men
and women used as tools can know.
Bent in the bean fields and hay fields,
bent by shingles carried up the roofer's
ladder, bent by the concrete mixer,
bent by the sledgehammer and shovel,
the jackhammer, the hoe and spade,
the engine block. His were palms
that knew other palms by their callouses
or lack of callouses. Knew my hands
were hands familiar with keyboards
and ballpoint pens, and understood
those were tools, too. Knew we all
were tools of war and power, tools of lust
and loss, tools that eventually lost
their use, grown weak from age,
rusted from neglect. When he asked me

to help with repairs after a storm,
I knew this was work he could no longer
do alone. I brought the tool box with me.
I handed him a hammer and waited
to follow his lead as I always had,
knowing sometimes trying is all
that's asked. Sharing the small losses
this tinkering with our hands can almost fix.

For Some Time After

The carpet burns against my back

        the lightbulbs cool to the touch

and there's something about ceiling fans
   I can't quit—dust like cigarette

      —the going-around
           sounds like my name

    chopped in your mouth
 when you split my legs

             on the floor beside the radiator

 —I still see blades spinning
        lavender behind closed eyes

phantom crawl of an emery board
       breath on my neck

               reaching for a glass already
        emptied

    the image of you
 standing in the doorway

    boxers to your knees

Vigil

Disability Day of Mourning 2019

No one has come to mourn us but ourselves.
A sparse crowd, a thin reminder.

We read the names aloud, the numbered tide
of filicide, the murders renamed mercy killings
by virtue of their victims.

Our lives, you remind us, unworthy of life.
And in the lists of names always the unnamed:

Baby girl 7-year-old girl 6-year-old boy Baby girl Girl 83-year-old woman Baby boy
4-year-old boy Boy 21-year-old man 30-year-old man 8-year-old boy 21-year-old
man 5-year-old boy Boy 20-year-old man 21-year-old man Baby boy Boy 6-year-old
girl 11-year-old girl 40-year-old man 16-year-old girl 37-year-old man 12-year-old
boy 68-year-old-woman 14-year-old girl 9-year-old boy 31-year-old man 5-year-
old girl 63-year-old man 83-year-old woman 56-year-old man 40-year-old woman
5-year-old girl 8-year-old boy 3-week-old baby 66-year-old man 9-month-old baby
69-year-old woman Baby boy

The never-ebbing tide.

And with each unnamed name, my throat
grows hollow, my voice unvoiceable.

Lay my body by the others, my brothers
and my sisters. Light the candle,
leave the calla.

This is no place for speech,
only for sorrow.

Gullah Babies

Granny and I were on our front porch shucking corn one day when I said, "Granny, there's a new boy at my school. His name's Mark." I smiled down at my lap, twisted a few strands of the corn silks around my pointer finger. "We're friends."

"He white or colored?" she asked.

Granny was in her seventies by that time, and she and the old folks on the island were the only ones I'd heard who used the word "colored." *White or colored? Colored or white?* The only thing that ever bothered me about Granny was that she was so hung up on race.

"He's black," I answered her.

A small glimmer of relief flashed across Granny's face as she reached up to adjust the red, orange, and yellow scarf tied around her head.

"He in the grade with you or older?"

"Same age as me. He's in my class." I sighed, trying to decide if just then was a good time to ask what needed asking. "Granny?" I began.

"What is it, Lena?"

"I was wondering, can Mark come over this weekend? He wants to see where I live."

She ripped away a corn husk and paused to look at me. With her dark brown fingers wrapped around the yellow corn, and the silks strewn over her wrist, Granny made a pretty picture.

"I reckon so," she said. "Are you gon' bring him to worship with us?"

Mark had said his parents were Catholics, and strict about it, too. Would they allow Mark to come to our church?

"I'll ask him," I said.

On Sunday, the day that Mark was supposed to come in on the ferry, rain was forecast. None of the houses on the island had paved yards or driveways, just loosely scattered gravel, sandy dirt, and grass. I was used to a mushy yard whenever it rained, but Mark was a town boy.

I would be embarrassed for him to get his feet all muddy in my yard.

I held my breath before I pulled my bedroom curtain back. But no such luck. Water had pooled up around the porch. Granny's Easter lilies were drowned. Rain ran off the eaves of my cousin Victoria's house and into a big puddle in her side yard. Vic's dog, Mitzie, a black lab, lay on their back porch. When Mitzie noticed me watching her from the window, she lifted her head and thumped her tail against the slatted floor of the porch.

I took a yellow sundress from my closet, one that Vic had given me last summer for my fifteenth birthday. Vic had sewn the dress from lightweight cotton fabric with light brown pinstripes running through it. The dress was the prettiest thing I owned, and I'd been saving it to wear for a special occasion.

I took the dress into the bathroom, showered and stepped into it. I walked into the kitchen to ask Granny's help with the zipper. Bacon sizzled on the stove, and flour dusted the counter.

The back screen door whined open and bumped closed. A second later, Vic came into the kitchen wearing a red raincoat.

Vic and I were only two months apart in age, which meant we'd both be turning sixteen that summer.

"Hey, y'all," Vic said as Granny zipped my dress. She came over and gave Granny a kiss on the cheek. Vic waited until after Granny had stepped into the bedroom, and then whispered to me, "Will he sleep in your bedroom tonight?"

"*What?*"

"Mark. Is he staying overnight?" Vic asked.

I almost swallowed my tongue at the idea of Mark sleeping with me. I said, "Why don't you ask Granny?"

"Hell no," Vic said. "She'd bust my ass with a whisk broom." Vic fingered her stubby, black braid. Her lilac-colored nails shone under the overhead light.

I sat down with her at the kitchen table. As I buttered a biscuit, someone tapped on the back door.

"Come in!" we both yelled.

Before the door opened I knew it was Jeremy Jensen, or JJ, as we called him. He'd promised to drive Vic and me over to the ferry. A tall, thin boy, JJ was two years older than us, and he'd just graduated high school the month before. He'd be shipping off to basic training for the army the next day. His leaving had been all anyone on our island had talked about for weeks. We all loved JJ. It was impossible not to. Quiet and thoughtful, he never said a bad word about anyone.

JJ came over to the table and looked down at me. I got a clear view of the scar underneath his chin, the one he'd gotten from falling off his bike when we were little. JJ was lighter skinned than me and his eyes were a lighter shade of brown.

He grabbed the bun at the nape of my neck and tugged on it. "Hey, Snaggle," he said.

I rolled my eyes at the old nickname. Once when I was six, I'd lost a tooth during a church dinner. Not knowing what to do with it, I'd leaned over and dropped it on JJ's dinner plate.

Though JJ wasn't from our island, his family had lived there and run the general store as long as I could remember. He was no blood relation to me the way Vic was, but he may as well have been.

JJ broke a biscuit in half. A layer of steam rose above his thumbs. He ate the biscuit in three big bites. I ate my bacon and a biscuit and stared out the kitchen window at the rain.

"C'mon, y'all. Ferry'll be coming in soon," JJ said.

I grabbed my umbrella and my leather sandals, put them in my oversize purse, slipped on a pair of rain boots, then followed Vic and JJ outside.

At least Vic had the good sense to wear a rain jacket with a hood; I cursed myself for leaving mine. My umbrella bent in on itself, and I got soaked. The rain poured so heavy I could hardly see. We piled into the truck's cab and just sat there, waiting for the rain to slow down. Water dripped into my eyes and rolled down my face and neck. Vic rooted around in the glove compartment and found some napkins for us to dry off with.

I'd wear my boots until we got to the ferry station, then I'd pull on the sandals and leave the mud-caked boots in Jeremy's truck. Back in fifth grade, on the very first day I'd boarded the mainland school bus, a white girl had looked at me and asked, "What's wrong with your shoes?" Shamed by her question, I looked down at my worn, unraveling shoelaces and at the little clumps of wet sand on my sneakers. I'd left a sandy path down the center aisle to my bus seat. Embarrassment caused tears to well behind my eyes.

As I grew older, I became more conscientious of how I looked to others. I couldn't run around wild-haired and barefooted off island the way I could at home. No more braless days or wrinkled shorts or muddy shoes for me.

Finally, the rain subsided and JJ inched us along toward the ferry dock. The main road leading toward the ferry was paved, but the driveways and side roads were all sand. The wipers made a comforting sound as a few drops of water splashed on the windshield.

Growing up on Pittman's Pointe, the only people I ever saw around the island were my own aunts, uncles, and cousins. And, of course, the "vacation people." The vacationers rented one of my cousin Florie's two camper trailers. They came to fish, ride on the bike trail over behind Florie's house, or just to have a secluded place to relax. Our island was one of the few along the coast that wasn't a commercial tourist resort, and we planned to keep it that way. My family owned about two-thirds of the land, and we prided ourselves on never selling. From the time I was little bitty, Granny and the old folks always said we didn't want to become another Tybee Island or a St. Simons, that we didn't want too many summer people coming in with noise and traffic.

When we got to the ferry, I didn't realize I'd forgotten to change my shoes until Mark stepped onto the platform and looked down at my muddy boots. His eyes traveled up to my face, and he smiled. Rain drizzled down on us; he wiped it from his brow.

Mark was very dark, like me. He had broad cheekbones and a strong chin.

"Did you have a nice ride over?" I asked him, after we'd said our hellos and begun to walk to the truck.

Mark looked around at the water and sand as though he were in a completely new world.

"Ferry ride took about fifteen minutes, just like you said. It's pretty here, so close to the water. How big is the island?"

The rain had cleared for a moment, and we all paused when we got to the truck.

"It's about four miles long and two miles wide," I told him. "JJ can ride us around a little after church."

"Let me guess," he said, smirking, "there's only one church, right?"

I nodded. "Fifty-four people live on the island."

"Fifty people!" Mark said. "Wow. You really do live in a nowhere swamp."

"It ain't a swamp," JJ said. "It's an island mostly full of woods and marshes."

If Mark noticed JJ's annoyed tone, he didn't show it. Instead, Mark asked, "Are you guys really inbred? At school they say everyone here is your cousin."

Something rolled over in my belly. I looked at JJ and then at Vic. Both waited, silently, to see how I'd respond.

"My mama's people are Pittmans," I explained to Mark. "But I'm related to everyone here in some way or other. I won't marry someone from the island, though." I said this last part with an eye roll: "I'm not inbred; none of us are."

I'd never known my daddy, but I didn't tell Mark that. I always hated explaining my family history to people because they usually looked at me with pity, especially when I explained that both my parents took off and left me to be raised by Granny.

We drove the main road home, straight across the middle of the island. Forest lined the highway for almost two miles, and then it gave way to open expanses of sand once we got closer to home.

"On the way to the ferry, we drove past the old slave block on the mainland. Did your family come in through there?" Mark asked me.

"Probably so," I told him.

"You ever want to research and find out? I mean, if I thought my folks were bought and sold here, I'd want to know."

I loved history as much as the next person, but I didn't want to research every little detail about my ancestors' suffering. Thelma Pittman, my great-grandmama, knew everything about the island. She could've told Mark anything he wanted to know. But I never took the opportunity to research anything. All I had were family stories. That was enough.

JJ answered for me: "I would *never* want to know where my folks were bought and sold." He looked pointedly at Mark.

Mark's brow furrowed with what I thought at first was anger, but then realized was just thoughtfulness.

I couldn't help but think that Mark had only come to the island to gawk at us. How had I not noticed what he was in school? Probably because I'd only known him two weeks. How silly of me to think I had any real idea of what sort of boy he was. Still, I tried to give him the benefit of the doubt. Maybe our lives were so foreign to him that he couldn't help but ask a passel of silly questions.

The smell of coffee greeted me as we walked in the kitchen door. Granny put out her hand to Mark. She said, "You the one from up north?"

Mark leaned toward her, a confused look on his face, and then looked at me. Granny repeated herself, and when he still didn't understand, Vic repeated Granny's words to him.

Everyone from our part of South Carolina understood Gullah accents, so no one we knew had trouble with Granny's speech. Mark's ignorance made me defensive. Was he judging her? As Mark ate the breakfast Granny had made, Granny stared at Mark, eyes squinted, biting her lower lip. Suspicious of outsiders to the point of paranoia, she always seemed annoyed with their questions.

As he buttered a second biscuit, Mark laid his shoulders back against his chair and said, "Delicious."

Granny grinned. She was the best cook on the island and knew it. When summer people came, everyone in the neighborhood recommended her special plate—peanut stew and yellow rice with red peas.

Mark asked, "Do you have police on the island?"

When I shook my head no, he asked, "So what would happen if there was a robbery or something?"

"You planning on robbing somebody while you're here?" JJ asked.

Mark grinned, said, "No, just curious."

Granny said, "We don't have much crime here. That Shackleford boy what lives over by the marsh took a grill off somebody's back porch one time, but his mama beat him so hard he carried it back."

Mark didn't say anything, and I wondered if he understood Granny.

JJ said, "This is a good place. I haven't heard about any crime since my family moved here."

"You're not from here?" Mark asked.

"My daddy was old army buddies with a guy from here. When the guy died, he left the general store on the island to my daddy. We moved here to run the store when I was five."

"Was it the store by the road we rode in on? The little blue building?"

"Yep, only general store on the island."

As we ate, JJ kept giving Mark the same squinty-eyed look that Granny had given him, that look of suspicion and distrust.

Like everything else on our island, the church was small. Made of white clapboard, it had a short steeple on top. Inside, a few pews lined each side of the altar. The pulpit held a big throne-like chair for our pastor, Ralph Means.

During church meeting that morning, Mark looked confused any time an older person spoke to him. Being from Boston, Mark occasionally had trouble with the Southern accents at our school, but Gullah seemed to puzzle him even more than a typical South Carolina accent.

We began devotional service with a spiritual hymn called "On My Journey Home," a call and response song. Usually, Deacon Sylvester Shackleford or his brother Charlie Shackleford led the song by singing a line or two. Then, we all joined in to repeat the words sung by the deacon. After we sang a few verses, we moaned our way through the rest of the song. The words were gibberish, but the intonations were pretty and soulful. I never thought of the song or the way we sang it as being odd or funny, but Mark got the giggles.

"This is the silliest song I ever heard," he whispered to me. "Sounds like those songs in old movies. I feel like we should all be out picking cotton."

Mark started moaning louder. When I raised my voice to meet his, he gave me a wink.

And because that wink was everything, I moaned even louder.

Mark leaned toward me, close enough to kiss and said, "I'm having fun."

Miss Eugenia, in the pew in front of us, stood and swayed from side to side, one hand raised toward the ceiling. Granny had told me that people waved their hands that way when they felt the spirit of God. The only strong feeling I'd ever had in church was a headache, especially when people shouted at the end of preaching.

Mark continued to moan loudly, and Miss Eugenia turned and looked at us. Her straw hat was angled slantwise over her forehead, a look that always gave her face a soft, elegant shape. She narrowed her eyes for a second, no doubt wondering why he was so loud.

I smiled at her. She returned the smile and faced forward again.

During preaching, Mark kept poking me and whispering. At one point, he described how he'd skinned his leg playing baseball the day before. "See," he said in a loud whisper, rolling up his pant leg to reveal a jagged scratch the length of my pinky. He pantomimed sliding into base. He stuck his arms out in front of us and bugged his eyes out. I laughed loudly, even though it wasn't all that funny.

Vic, who sat on my other side, patted me lightly on the forearm. "Y'all hush," she whispered.

But it was too late.

From behind the pulpit, Reverend Means said, "I wish y'all would be quiet back there, young people."

Half the congregation turned to look at Mark and me.

I looked at Granny, who sat in her usual space near the pulpit. Because I never got into much trouble, Granny seldom punished me. Whenever I did some little thing she disapproved of—scored less than an A on a test or skipped church—she let me know it by her expression.

Just then, she squeezed her lips together. A muscle twitched in her jaw.

After preaching, I told Granny that us kids were taking Mark down to the beach. She nodded but wouldn't look at me. I knew she'd wait until Mark was long gone on the ferry that afternoon before giving me a talking to. Granny wasn't the sort to berate me in front of everyone.

There were two wide beaches on the island, and we chose the one on the north island because of its proximity to the church. The boys went down to the surf. Vic and I sat on the little plank porch, the one Granny always said my great granddaddy had built. I felt proud whenever I sat on it. Though I'd never known Great Granddaddy Pittman, sitting at this place he'd made with his own hands made me feel close to him. I wondered if he was a romantic like me, someone who liked to lie back and look out at the water and think about love and the future.

"Can't believe you and Mark were so loud during meeting," Vic said.

"He was telling me about a baseball game."

"I heard. Whole church did." She looked out at Mark. He and JJ had rolled up their pant legs and were standing in the surf. "He's judging us," she said. "He's been judging us all day. And for that I don't like him, but he's your friend, your soon-to-be boyfriend, so the only person who has to like him is you."

Mark took off his shirt and jogged up to the porch to lay it on the bench, the only dry place around. "Hey, Lena," he said. "Ever skinny-dip?"

I looked at Vic, who bit back a smile.

I shook my head no.

"You scared?" Mark asked.

"No."

"Then why not?" he asked.

JJ came over to hear what we were talking about.

"Says she won't skinny-dip," Mark told JJ.

"Smart girl," JJ said.

Mark pulled off his shorts and flung them onto the porch rail. He took off running toward the water, then trudged through it, ankle-deep, wearing only his underpants.

The three of us threw back our heads and laughed.

"Cute butt!" I called after him.

"What butt?" Vic asked. "He's got nothing back there."

Once he was waist high in the water, Mark turned back and shouted, "C'mon in." He looked straight at me when he said it. For a moment, there was only the two of us. His smile. His confidence. My heart, thumping so hard I felt it in my rib cage.

Everything about Mark made me want to be defiant and carefree, the same as he was. I stood and reached back to unzip my dress.

"What are you doing?" JJ asked.

"Oh, come on. It'll be fun. Don't you want to try something different?" I got the dress halfway unzipped, then leaned back toward Vic for her help.

"Why are you doing this?" she asked, her hands in her lap.

"You two can be sticks in the mud. I want to have fun."

Becoming more frustrated with the dress, I pulled my arms out of it, then twisted it around so the zipper faced me. I stepped out of the dress and left it there on the porch. I didn't dare take off my bra and underwear. I wasn't that bold, or that crazy.

Out in the water, Mark grabbed my head and dunked me under, which pissed me off because I didn't want my hair wet.

"Let's race to that little strip of land," he said, pointing to an isle about a hundred yards out.

It was a tiny little grassy knoll. I'd never swum that far. No one I knew had ever dared.

"Scared?" he asked.

When I hesitated, he said, "We could race."

Without waiting for my answer, he drew in a big breath and dove under.

I looked back at Vic and JJ. One of them had picked up my dress and hung it neatly on the porch rail. The dress and Mark's shorts whipped back and forth in the breeze.

After several seconds, Mark still had not surfaced. I was just about to go under and hunt for him when he came up a few feet to my right.

"I think we better head back. Looks like rain," I said, pointing up at the clouds.

"Nah, a little rain won't hurt us," he said. "Come race me. Please, baby?"

He'd never called me baby before.

I wondered how long it would take me to swim out to the isle. I was a strong swimmer, had been since I was a little girl. And wasn't Mark my guest? I wanted him to have fun. So far, all we'd done was eat breakfast and go to Sunday meeting. He'd never want to come back here.

He'd never want to spend time with boring old me ever again.

"I'll do it," I said.

He smiled big at me. "Ready?"

I made sure my arms were level with his. He kept inching his body forward, and I did the same.

"Get set," he said.

A raindrop hit my forehead and ran down my nose. Little drops sprinkled my arms and shoulders.

"Go!" he yelled, taking off, splashing water back into my face.

He had a head start, but once I'd swum half a dozen breast strokes I came level with him. I focused on breathing and thrusting. Kicking. From the corner of my eye, his dark shape began to slow, or maybe I was moving better once I'd gotten warmed up. I closed my eyes. Pretty soon I developed a rhythm.

Breathe. Thrust. Kick.

Breathe. Thrust. Kick.

When my eyes opened again, I was pretty close to the isle, but when I looked to my right, I didn't see him anywhere. Still moving forward, I turned my head left.

No Mark. No sign of him.

I stopped swimming and looked back. It was a wonder how far I'd come. The sky had gone completely grey. Rain came down steadily. Though it was still early afternoon, the overcast sky had created a twilight.

Then, I saw Mark pull himself from the water and walk up the beach. He must've been over a hundred yards away. Through the rain and grey twilight, the distance seemed somehow farther than it had originally been. I became aware of what a stupid thing I'd done, like that time I climbed a tree, kept climbing higher and higher to see how far I could go. Finally, when I looked down, I was stunned by the space between my body and the ground. The tops of the houses were all patched, and I could see clear to the ferry dock and the church.

When they saw me stop in the water, Vic and JJ waved. How far away they were. Their tiny shapes sat on the porch, shielded from the rain. I couldn't tell if they were cheering me on or asking, "What the hell?!" Probably the latter.

Mark had given up. But I wouldn't. I'd prove I could do something he didn't have the guts to do.

I started swimming toward the little isle again. This time much slower, knowing that it wasn't a race anymore. It was about endurance and courage, not speed. I stopped several times and looked, in awe, to my left and right. Nothing but water as far as my eyes could see. The water and sky were both grey, and looking out on the horizon I could barely distinguish the line that separated the grey water from the grey sky. In the spaces all around me, rain pebbled the ocean, coming down and then pinging back up, like raindrops falling off the eaves of a house into a puddle.

When I was within about twenty feet of the isle, I saw movement to my left. I looked over, and there was JJ.

He grabbed me by the arm, but the rain coming down all around us was so loud I couldn't hear what he was telling me. His fingers dug into my arm, a persistent grip that annoyed me. Dragging me behind him, he turned and began to tread water. I wrenched away, turned around and quickly swam those last twenty feet. My fingers brushed the grainy side of the isle.

When I turned to swim back to the beach, I was instantly struck by JJ's face. I paused a moment to watch him. He'd always been a passive and reserved boy, but just then I saw the most intense look I'd ever seen on his face. He stared at me, his lips pressed together, head angled down so that his chin grazed the water. It was like he wasn't JJ at all. Did he hate me? Or was it anger on his face, an anger that was turning to hatred?

We began to swim back at a frantic pace. At one point, I felt our bodies synchronize, or maybe I just imagined it.

Lightning lit the sky. I felt a wave wash over my head, knocking me under for a moment. I resurfaced, blubbering and spitting out water. About halfway to shore, I turned back to see a larger wave coming at me. That time, I was able to at least hold my breath before I went under.

JJ pulled himself from the water and turned to look over his shoulder for me. I rode the last wave in and allowed it to wash me ashore. As he ran toward the covered porch, I turned back again. How lucky I was to get back in time. For the most part, we'd been swimming with the current on the way back. As I watched the water rising a dozen feet above the little isle, I knew there was no way I could've fought the current and won.

The rain came down steadily just then. Through the twilight and the sheets of falling water, I could see that Mark was doubled over. Vic knelt in front of him, examining something on his foot.

As I climbed the plank steps under the porch canopy, I heard JJ ask, "What happened?"

"There was a broken bottle in the sand. He gashed his foot on it," Vic told us.

"Can you walk on it?" JJ asked.

Mark stood, but as soon as he put weight on the foot, he winced and sat down again. Blood gushed from the cut and onto the porch planks.

JJ pointed down the beach. "Lena, go run down to Mr. Mason's. Call an ambulance to meet us on the mainland ferry dock. Tell Mason to let us borrow his boat."

I froze for a second, and he said, "Go on! Hurry up, girl!"

I turned, flew down the porch steps and took off running down the beach. My wet hair was plastered against my face.

I must've made it to Uncle Lonnie's house in about three minutes. I burst through the door, breathless.

"What is it, child?" Lonnie's wife, Karen, asked me.

"Is Uncle Lonnie here? My friend cut his foot on a bottle at the beach. It's gushing blood. We need to ferry him over to the mainland."

She looked down at me. No doubt she'd seen quite a lot of my skin before. I'd worn two-piece swimsuits to the beach since primary school. But my outfit just then—the soggy cotton panties and the faded old push-up bra—was enough to make her pause and frown.

"He down at the store. The keys is on the counter over there. You need me to ride with y'all?"

I grabbed the keys. "I-I don't know. I guess."

She came over and put her hand on mine, took the keys away. "C'mon, child," she said. She went over to the phone and called the ambulance.

We drove Lonnie's truck down to the beach. When they saw the truck, the three of them came up the hill toward us—Vic and JJ on either side of Mark, who had one arm slung around each of their shoulders for support. His bad foot was raised, and he hopped on his good one. Once JJ helped him into the back of the truck, Karen drove back to her house and we all loaded into the motor boat. As she steered us through the water, she called out to JJ, "Look in that plastic bag and give him some of that antiseptic spray."

JJ did as he was told and sprayed Mark's foot with the medicine.

Vic handed me my sundress and sandals. As I slipped them on, I caught JJ's eye. He'd been staring at me, but when he caught me looking he turned his attention back to Mark's foot.

When we got to the ferry dock, the ambulance was already sitting there waiting for us.

Karen told JJ and Vic to take the boat home. "We'll call Lonnie to pick us up later," she said.

Karen and I rode in back of the ambulance with Mark.

Mark's mama, Mrs. Miller, met us in the emergency waiting room. I'd never met her before, yet I knew her as soon as I saw her. She had the same deep-set eyes as Mark, the same tall, lanky body. She kept looking down at my dress, which was mostly dry, except

for the places where my wet underwear dampened it. My sand-encrusted feet made my skin look ashy.

"You don't have to wait here with me," Mrs. Miller said to us. She hoisted her shoulder bag up. "I've got it from here, thank you."

I wondered if Mrs. Miller blamed us for Mark's accident. Would Mark blame us?

Karen touched her shoulder, but Mrs. Miller looked down at Karen's hand and frowned.

As we exited the emergency room doors, Karen said, "I don't know why it's so important for those uppity folks to like you."

We missed the last ferry, so Karen called Uncle Lonnie to pick us up. When we finally got back to the island, Lonnie offered to drive me home, but I told him I'd rather walk.

The rain had cleared away. The cloudless sky created the perfect backdrop for the white gulls that flew overhead. As I walked past the other island neighborhood, Water Haven, with its porch lights and moss-covered trees, I could see the blue store ahead. There was something very comforting about going to the blue store and talking with JJ while he swept floors and stocked shelves. I'd miss that once he moved away.

Inside the blue store, Sylvester Shackleford and his brother Charlie were playing checkers. They sat on barstools against a wall by the register.

"Hey, guhl," they greeted me.

JJ was stocking a cooler with Cokes and juices. I sat down on one of the little stools in front of the register and waited for him to come around. After about ten minutes of watching the Shackleford brothers' checkers game, I looked back to see JJ just standing there, watching me. He turned back to the cooler and muttered something.

"Just came to tell you the news about Mark. He needed stitches but he'll be fine."

"I figured as much. People don't usually die from a cut on the foot," he said.

I went over and poked him in the ribs.

"*Damnit*, Lena. Quit it!"

I didn't realize I was backstepping until my elbow banged against a shelf.

The Shackleford brothers went silent, watching us. I grinned at them, trying to make light of everything.

Though the cooler was full to bursting with drinks, JJ stood there with his hand on the door, as though he had more work to do. After a moment, I saw that it wasn't the drinks he was looking at. Instead, he used the glass door as a mirror to watch me.

I stared at his back a moment, until I realized he wanted me to leave. He wasn't cruel enough to say it, but I got the message just the same.

"See you later," I said, looking in the direction of the Shackleford brothers.

"Bye," they said.

The next day, everyone held a farewell party for JJ. He was set to start basic training the following week, and he'd be flying out of Charleston that night.

I didn't go to JJ's farewell party. Instead, I watched from my bedroom window seat, hugging a fluffy pillow to my chest. Through the window, I could see all the well-wishers— Old Miss Mason, back slightly stooped as she grinned her toothless, dimpled smile; the youngest Mason girl in a dress that kept lifting around her knees as she twirled; and Delia Shackleford, the sweetest woman in the world, who wouldn't let JJ leave without handing him an envelope full of church money she'd collected.

Someone had strung tea lights around the porch railing of the blue store, brightening what was already the brightest building on the island. Lonnie and Karen's house sat two houses down on the right. People moved back and forth between the blue store and Karen's house, the site of the barbecue.

I lifted the window halfway, so I could smell everything. Uncle Lonnie Mason made a barbeque sauce with a twinge of garlic and hot pepper. It always tasted sweet and tangy. I could smell that, along with the tender meat that I knew was falling off the bones. That's how they did it on our island. They cooked the pig over charcoals in an open pit. Lonnie and Karen—one or the other, or maybe both—had sat out with the pig all night, swathing it in sauce and turning the bits of flesh over until it grew so tender you could easily break it apart in your hands.

That morning, Granny and Vic had gone over to Karen's to steam crabs and make a peanut stew.

My mouth watered, and I put my nose down to the window screen and breathed in. My stomach moaned for a plate of pulled pork on a bed of Charleston yellow rice.

JJ cut through our yard on his way out to the blue store. I slid back from the window so he wouldn't see me. He stood in our yard, peering at the door, as though waiting for something.

Me?

Then, someone I couldn't see called JJ's name. Looking over his shoulder, he called back to them and laughed.

My nine-year-old cousin Damian took my bike off the front porch. I heard the wheels bump against the porch steps as he rolled it down. Then, his little snot-nosed self rode it out toward the blue store.

I sat in the window all afternoon, looking out, and occasionally flipping channels on the TV.

Around 6:45, JJ's old truck lumbered down the sandy road between my house and Vic's.

I knew he was headed out to catch the last ferry.

He halted for a second in front of the house, the engine rumbling as it idled.

I knew that for the rest of my life I'd never be as comfortable with anyone as I was with Vic and JJ. No one really knows you unless he knew you as a child. A new friend would not have memories of me putting my bloody tooth on his dinner plate, or swimming in sync with me during a summer storm.

Most of the well-wishers had gone inside the blue store to laugh and tell stories; the others had gone home, carrying plates of barbecue and seafood and stew. Somehow, I knew this time was meant for JJ and me. I was supposed to go to him, or maybe he should have come to me. That's how it *should* have been, but neither was to be.

His eyes found my silhouette in the window. He raised a hand in passing. I stared as he pulled onto Ferry Road, and I watched his taillights disappear into the trees.

Sonnet

If I say I am an American it will suddenly be clear
I do not know what   grain I am working

against. What begins underneath the other
side is folly   almost is news   almost as

what we already know or should know   dances
in headlines before us. Anybody looking for an anecdote

can dote on the old barns dotting the landscape so
profusely. Anybody looking for a properly licensed technician   will

want to dip a toe into crystal creeks.
We are busy turning

the words we nearly hear   nearly as hairy
as sumac and who doesn't   want that.

Who doesn't want the comingled juices of   our anthems blowing through their
    valves like
wild lights that are shining from   selectively crepuscular stars.

Buzz Off

This was never going to add to our cup. It's raining.
Let's go indoors. The place is so small not everybody

is going to fit. So,   who wants to leave? I mean
just because we all came out doesn't mean any of us

should stay. Especially since our drinks are flat.
Imagine a claw that pays for itself. This compels us.

In worn legends we are walking backward. By we
I mean you   and I. Whatever is wanting to split

an enemy's heart cannot be allowed to persist. If
they are less careful, lies   will pile up behind a move.

It will be like love without a single sinuous rill. My
enemy is as dear as access to simultaneous platforms.

The River

By cliffs, in the room of morning, soft data
blew like a weeping wildfire. Nobody believed it,
so it died and then quickly reanimated as
an emblem abandoned near a modest, well-kept
villa. Similarly, you have already drifted into the first
stage and, now, might as well fill your rainboots.

I am looking over the railing with you at mint.
It grows profusely, almost unnaturally, as we swim
through its scent, which has been unlocked by
a waxing sun. All of this reminds me of the time
an absolute stranger pressed a vision into the minds
of everybody in our vicinity. We laughed, dustily,

as it happened. Probably this is half predictable
considering how we kept encountering, as we ventured
deeper and deeper into the proverbial woods, new,
but empty, snail shells. Those shells only left us asking
ourselves and each other, Where are the snails?
If you look the other way, you will see me looking

at you from a simultaneous dimension. You will
feel the pulse of my efforts as a comforting thing,
and, feeling it, will recognize it as your own. Still,
nothing is closer to what matters than what is inherent
in what already exists. What already exists rises along
a vector of curious tenderness. If, atop a tall pylon,

the mother of a brood of goslings begins feeling
restless about passing humans, it might be time to
leave their nest and enter the larger safety of the river.
There, hawks may descend, talons slicing through
eponymous air, and wild dogs may howl their hungers
into the starry panorama of a semi-navigable night.

Run Away With Me

I've always been stuck in the past, frozen somewhere in high school when I didn't know how I felt about you. We've come a long way, Alex, and I don't like thinking everyone is growing up without us. I don't know how everyone is getting married all of a sudden. I walked into Belk the other day and saw Courtney and her boyfriend registering for their wedding. It's not that I think that Courtney and her boyfriend—fiancé—are a bad match because of miscegenation—I like that word, it's a pretty word—I just don't like their relationship. When we were friends, she accidentally sent me this long stream of text messages meant for him, and in the messages she talked about how tiny his penis was and how she hoped it would be bitten off by a whale when he became a marine biologist. Later, she changed her mind and cried and apologized for cheating, but said that he had cheated first—I don't know, her story really confused me.

I could never be in love the way Courtney loves her fiancé. I could never forgive someone who cheated on me and yelled at me, and who I felt I needed to yell at in return. I get what you meant about them though. People do give them looks around these parts—especially when they're downtown, holding hands. There's a lot of change going on, with the streets being paved over and banners hung from every lamppost in town to signal changes in season. I wouldn't want us to be here if we had worked out, getting hot dogs from the country store or helping renovate the old mill for some new art space. These places wouldn't want us, either. Brooke—my sister, not the girl we went to school with—doesn't like where the town's going, says that no matter how much they try and make the town over we can't ever change its heart. Brooke is a very strong advocate of interracial marriage, even though it's been legal here for over twenty years. She goes on rants about it and often her face will turn red because she's not getting enough oxygen or her blood pressure is too high. I know that she would protect us, too, but that doesn't matter much to you, does it? You've got bigger things to be afraid of, things Brooke can't help us with, and I get that.

Sometimes I worry Brooke will have to have an abortion, something else that's frowned upon around here. I don't know where she would go to have an abortion. There aren't any Planned Parenthoods. She's such a large girl, with all that curly hair, and she seems to throw herself and her vagina at any guy who wants to have sex. All guys want to have sex. That's something I've found out in the worst way.

You're mad at me, and I figured I'd explain how things were so you'd be less mad. I think you're mad because you think I gave it up to some other guy, or because I left you somehow, but both of those things aren't really true. Word travels fast in this town, which is why I've been careful to only tell people outside the city limits and on narrow dirt roads that jerk and jolt you as you bump along them. It's best to keep our innermost thoughts settled at the bottom of the pond in front of my grandfather's house or outside the entrance to the country club.

This spring, I met a boy on one of those gay applications I download on my phone, the ones you used to always frown at me about. I only downloaded them for conversation, and the dick pics just flooded in for forty days and nights, and nothing was cleansed like in the Bible. I felt dirty from it all until I met the boy. I won't tell you his real name. I will tell you this: he was six foot three inches tall and broad shouldered, and he was heavier than me but in a thick, muscular way. He took me to coffee and I kept checking my phone to see if you would call. The boy, who I will call Jonathan because that is a plain, universally anonymous name, asked me if I wanted to come over to his house to play video games. I had no idea this meant have sex. You know I had no idea this meant have sex. I have steered away from sex for so long.

I stopped by Jonathan's house on a Saturday afternoon when I knew my parents wouldn't ask where I was going. I was tired of their noseyness. They really needed to worry about Brooke, who is probably pregnant already and needs an abortion. I walked into the house and Jonathan asked me to take off my shoes like he was Asian and super zen. I don't really even know what "zen" means. My shoes were the first thing to come off until I got to the couch. Jonathan was shirtless already, and he had a six-pack and it was nice, but I tried not to stare because that's rude.

"You want something to drink?" he asked me.

I didn't know what to say. I was thirsty, as Brooke would term it, for a lot of things. I asked for a Coke and Jonathan didn't move. Instead he reached and began touching my privates, on top of and then under my clothes.

I don't know why you don't want to talk about this. I don't know what's wrong with you these days. You're so glum. You could use some Prozac, I bet, or whatever Dr. Jenkins is giving out like free candy. You act like this happened to you, like you're the victim here. You know you're mentally ill, right? You know you need more help than me. I wish you would stop talking about how I need help, always mumbled under your breath.

Sorry to sound so accusatory. I know you don't mean to hurt me. I know you're only looking to help in your own way, and I know that I must have hurt you but I don't understand how. I'm the one with the black-and-blue face, fading green and yellow now, and you are the one with a girlfriend and a scholarship to a state college.

Why are you angry with me?

Jonathan and I took off the rest of our clothes together because I wanted to. I wanted to see what it was like to have a boy touch me and kiss me and want me in an absolutely sexual way. I needed a clearer definition of wanting outside of what we were, which has always been something in between friends and soulmates, lovers and strangers. I wanted to see what it was like to have someone so tall lumber over me, but I didn't expect it to hurt so much, that sort of affection. Who have you hurt like that? Deep in the night when you wake up wanting and roll over on top of them, who do you hurt?

I shoved at him because it hurt so badly. I didn't want him in me that way. I thought I might be damaged internally. I tried to sit up but he ground me back down, and maybe I should have started the story earlier at a happy place—maybe I should have started the story here:

You and me, sitting in a diner, my neck crooked but not in a broken way. I was staring at you in the best way, like it was the morning after sex, but really all we'd done was lay in each other's arms and watch movies. I didn't have to tell you I didn't want to have sex with you while you had a girlfriend. I didn't have to tell you what our limits were. You understood them even though they were unspoken. The sunlight caught on your face, made your hair gleam almost white, and your eyes sparkled like a lake. Please tell me you remember this, because I'm about to talk about what happened when I showed up at your door.

I chose the side door because I knew you'd answer. My face was swelling and I was bleeding from the mouth. I reached up and touched my face gingerly while I waited, wanting to see how far I could push myself before it hurt. I had been pushing and hurting myself for days, weeks, months, I realized, and I'd gotten to this point. I couldn't go home. Brooke would be outraged and want revenge. She was feisty like that, with her bleached tips and fang-like teeth, ready to bite into anyone who hurt me.

When you saw me, you just stood there. That was something like I'd expected. You were in shock. Your girlfriend was upstairs. You walked out onto the side porch and shut the door behind you.

"What happened?" you asked.

"He was supposed to get me a Coke," I said.

You reached out, just for a moment, like you were going to touch my face. You would have touched it softly. But you stopped. "Who did this to you?"

I stuttered my words. I don't know how to write out stuttering on paper. I'll try my best. "W-we w-were d-doing s-stuff." I don't know if I stuttered every word, but that was the general effect.

"Do you need to go to the hospital?" you asked.

"No, Alex," I said, but my mouth was so numb I could barely say your name.

I shifted on the side porch. I didn't know what to do. I didn't know what you wanted me to do. The moon was coming out, yellow like it was infected with something. Bugs buzzed in the air but I didn't bother swatting them away. I wanted to go home. I wanted to go in your house. I wanted to hide in your room.

You walked back upstairs and told your girlfriend you'd be back in a minute. I could hear the two of you discussing something, probably me, then arguing. I don't know if she knows the truth. I don't know what the truth is, really, about us, about you. That seems much too complicated for me to put my finger on at the moment.

You drove me to the hospital in your pickup truck. You stopped at the ER entrance and had to help me kick the side door open. It gets stuck every now and then. The night was glistening just like your eyes had that day in the diner, and it made me sad. I realized I was crying and I want you to know I was crying because we had a story. I want you to know that whatever our story was, it was ours. That sounds so cheesy, but it's the most I'd ever hoped for, to share anything with you at all.

In the ER lobby, I saw a girl I mistook for Brooke sitting behind the receptionist desk. Brooke is sometimes a receptionist at the hospital. She works night shifts because she has nothing to do with her life other than have sex with guys. It's really the saddest thing in the world. Sadder than me and you, possibly.

I was ushered back into a room and I waited a while for a doctor to come see me. Courtney was my nurse, ironically enough, just long enough to see my face and ask what had happened. I didn't know what to say. People knew I was gay. They had to. People knew who I was, but she had seen me with you before, I was sure, and I didn't want to implicate you. I didn't want people with their torches walking through town toward your house. I didn't want someone to knock on the side door to your house and just shoot you to death.

I'm always looking out for you. Whether you know it or not. Do you remember when you invited me to chess club and I said yes only for you to drop out the next week and play soccer? I stayed in chess club so I could learn how to beat you at the game we've been playing for years. But I never got very good.

The whole time I was being doctored, I thought of the way you'd looked at me. Like you understood exactly what had happened and it was beyond disapproval—it was betrayal. But at what point would I have been yours? When we were seventy and able to relax in a home together? When I was a wrinkled, giant prune, or when I'd amassed enough diseases to demand a free health clinic in town?

We are a small town. Not a ghost town, although there are plenty of ghosts, all walking amongst the new people I don't recognize. People talk here, in the café they opened beside the old pharmacy, in the checkout line at the grocery store. People are going to talk about me, and I'm going to sacrifice to make sure no one knows what we are and what we meant to each other, and the truth is even I don't know what we meant to each other, just the mountains of feelings you made me move and how often you said you loved me. I will stay in, keep to myself, make excuses when Brooke wants to go to the movies.

"Why're you protecting him?" you asked me before I climbed out of the truck.

I won't go into rape statistics, or how many rapists are actually prosecuted, but the number is small. The number is not in my favor. And, really, more importantly, I don't want people knowing things didn't go how I wanted. Everyone from Brooke to sad, knowing Courtney realizes how I wanted you, how I've wanted you since sixth grade. The bus trip to the zoo where you fed the orangutan that got way too angry. The way you smiled so I could count all your teeth. It was like knowing every single one of your secrets.

I might have said something like "Leave me alone" but my mouth was too swollen.

They diagnosed me with herpes some weeks later, when it first flared up, and I cried because I knew that you'd be so disappointed in me. I knew that you really wouldn't want me like this. I asked the nurses to keep it a secret even though I knew they liked to gossip with their husbands and children and soon everyone would know. Your father is one of the doctors at the family medicine center in town, and I knew he would be so disappointed in me too, and I wondered if he would wonder about you in a different way from how I wondered about you. I wondered if he wondered about you at all.

I haven't seen Jonathan since. I promise. I haven't drunk Coke since. I have lain in bed and tried to figure out where I went wrong in the grander scheme of things. I am still unsure if there was a time when I could have stopped you, made you stand in place, let you be less of a man and more of the Alex I've always known and loved even when I didn't know it. I just don't think we could have been those people here, in this town, and I thought maybe we might have left at some point together, but you're gone now, and I'm still here, behind you always.

I will go to Courtney and her fiance's wedding and watch from the shadow of willow trees. I will think about how I wanted to run away with you. I will ruminate on all the ways we could have made each other happy, but you are a fantasy, and I am a drone bomb.

When the HIV test came back negative, Brooke hugged me and cried and then slapped me in the face. "You need to tell me who he *is*," she said.

I mimicked zipping my lips shut, locking them, and throwing away the key.

I'd rather not let anyone know that someone who's not you can hurt me this much. It's just a preference of mine.

And now, back to you.

How's your girlfriend? How's school going? I hope it's great. I hope you are still with her and not sleeping around. That would make me sadder, and I don't know why. It would feel like you're slipping away even more.

I decided to take a semester off to recuperate. It might not have been the best idea since now I have too much time to think.

I hope you're not doing anything too crazy, like trying krokodil tears. I hear people do that at college, when they're all grown up.

Be safe is what I mean. Don't make me come and save you.

Elegiac Advice Unwanted

I bought her a pair of Superstar Adidas
but they weren't what she wanted.
From her favorite spot I brought fajitas
but that's exactly what her aunt did.

I don't pretend to know what she's thinking.
If it's true, as she claims, life's a kind of trial
then she should try, at least, to stop drinking.
Diffuse her pain by attempting to smile.

When she insists she won't get better,
I suggest even orphaned sparrows sing.
When she's this upset she says to let her
be. *It's just like a man to try and fix things.*

But if the roof is leaking you have to patch it.
If the bathroom's flooding, turn off the faucet.
Your dog runs off. You don't attempt to catch it.
Aren't you responsible for having lost it?

At the Diagnosis

They tell me things about my body that I do not know,
that I cannot see or feel, that I cannot verify—
even as they scroll through my CT scan on the monitor
which looks like cloudy weather to me and not like organs
inside my body or inside the transparent man model
I remember from high school biology. They tell me
cancer grows in my dark recesses, point to the black oval
on the scan, which I think looks like a clearing in the clouds.
I think I feel fine and I tell them I have never felt
better, healthier, more fit, and they say it is often
asymptomatic, without symptoms, they say, until it
has grown too large and spread too far to treat. They say the tumor
squats inside me, that it will kill me from inside if they
do not save me. I imagine a rat, gnawing through organs,
but I think I would feel that, and then I remember stories
of women having babies when they had not known they were
pregnant, of women having melon-sized masses removed
and I think of melons sprouting inside me, maybe
from watermelon seeds I swallowed as a child
on summer afternoons. The surgeon is talking about
surgery, about cutting unseen enemies and organs
out of me. He shows me what he will remove on a wall chart
that does look like high school biology. The oncologist
talks about chemo and radiation, depending
on what surgery reveals. I am nodding and a nurse
or scheduler or assistant comes in with forms to sign
and appointments and instructions and I am on the train.

Paradise was consumed

one night in early November

The feast lasted several hours

No one made that up

You can't foment metaphors
as good as the unchartered

Birch before oak
sleuth bewitched
shoreline glazed

Spate of ash can minutiae
colonic ferryman throat
left eye metal switchback
a machete confession

The House of Forgetting

The rift between Toby and his mother happened in her garage, a place she used to store memories, not her car. He went there looking for her, looking for a way to separate himself from her. A narrow path wound through towers of cardboard boxes splitting open to reveal scraps of cloth, yellowing papers, and the water-stained bindings of old books. He stepped around a loom half-strung with dusty wool and stumbled against a steamer trunk upholstered in molding leather. Both the loom and trunk had been added to the garage since the last time he visited. "Family heirlooms," she would have said if he asked her, but he knew they were the castoffs of some other family, bargains discovered at an auction or flea market.

When he was growing up, she took him to yard sales every summer weekend. "You'll know," she'd say, trailing her fingers over other people's discarded toasters and dented lampshades. "When something belongs with you, you'll feel it." The sheets on his bed were worn soft before he ever touched them, their mismatched plates had chips missing, and the water marks of other people's mugs ringed their kitchen table, but he and his mother had none of the stories that went with the history of their objects. "It's better that way," she told him. "We'll make the stories to suit ourselves." He'd agreed with her because reality had felt no more permanent than smoke, a few words enough to waft it away. They created a grandmother who crocheted afghans for every birthday and cousins who handed down worn jeans and sweatshirts. Magnets from the Grand Canyon covered their refrigerator, a conch shell rested on their end table, and they shook salt and pepper from miniature lighthouses: all souvenirs of vacations taken by other people and then adopted by his mother. She had a story for every object and every story started with "remember when." For his eleventh birthday she gave him a baseball trophy engraved with someone else's name and a story of home runs and sweaty team practices to replace the reality of a solitary summer spent rereading comic books in his bedroom, but she never made up a father for him. Even for his mother some things couldn't be transformed and were better left forgotten.

For twenty-four years he remembered the stories she told him to remember and forgot the ones that made her sad, but on that day in the garage he meant to tell her he was done. "The stories you tell about our life aren't true," he meant to say. "You steal from other people's lives."

Afterward he couldn't remember if he had said those words and, if so, what she had said in response. He had battled through the detritus of the garage to find her and then he had fought his way out. As he left he tripped over a box of empty yogurt containers. His arm went through the back of a rotting wicker chair; when he pulled free, a protruding nail carved a long furrow into his forearm. The varnish on the chair frame had felt sticky and the wood had creaked under his weight. Those sense impressions felt like hummocks of grass at the edge of a swamp: safe enough to bear his weight and keep him from plunging into the muddy water that lay beneath.

During the six-hour drive back to his apartment, clusters of raindrops spattered his windshield, squalls that ended almost before they began. Wind whisked autumn leaves into whorls of russet and yellow blowing across the highway. Tender hives bloomed on the soft skin of his abdomen and underarms. The sky seemed near enough to touch, as if he drove through a world made of air. He held onto the edges of that day and let the center of it slip away.

Four years earlier Toby had completed an associate's degree and found a job as a medical technician one state over from where he'd grown up. It pleased him to live in a different state from his mother, the geographic separation standing in for the emotional distance that he couldn't achieve. At the lab where Toby worked, blood and tissue arrived in glass vials and small plastic containers labeled with bar codes and numbers. When he logged the samples into a computer, the numbers linked to names that trailed a history of blood pressure readings, weight, and cholesterol levels. Sometimes there were notes—"complained of recurring abdominopelvic discomfort" or "palpated approximate 5 mm inguinal swelling"—but the words were no better than the numbers at telling the stories of the people who had submitted to having pieces of themselves trimmed away in a search for answers. His job required him only to process these small offerings from their bodies with efficiency and competence, but he tried to be gentle as he sliced the tissue samples into translucent sheets, then affixed them to glass slides; sometimes he added chemical stains to the tissue until it bloomed fuchsia and blue, revealing its secrets to the doctors who received the trays of slides that he created. The lab had long stainless steel counters, walls the color of chicken broth, and tall stools that rolled on wheels. An autoclave stood ready to steam blades and tweezers into sterility. A row of centrifuges emanated a low hum as they spun blood into its component parts. At work he wore latex gloves; when he peeled them off to eat his lunch, the soft intimacy of bread against skin felt illicit.

The day after the argument his coworker, Julie, leaned against the lab counter next to him. "You doing okay?" she asked. They were about the same age, but she was married and had a two-year-old son. She handled the slides with neat, economical movements and never got distracted in the middle of a task.

"Yeah, I'm fine," he said. His face felt puffy and fragile, as if his memories were trying to crawl outside of his skin.

On the day of the argument the sound of his mother's humming had guided him through the maze of other people's cast-off possessions to where she perched on a stool at the back of the garage. Pages torn from back issues of National Geographic *and* Woman's Day *covered the folding table beside her and the floor was littered with scraps of paper. When he found her she smiled at him, her eyes made small and sly by the glasses perched on her nose.*

Julie's hand hovered over his shoulder as if she was thinking of touching him but wasn't sure if she should. The indecisive gesture was uncharacteristic and made him feel guilty, like he had failed to be the person she expected him to be.

"Just tired," he added. "I didn't sleep well last night."

His mother had held out a picture, a page ripped from a catalog. "Look, I'm making a memory for you," she said. A metal lockbox filled with photos stood open on the table next to her. "No more memories," he'd wanted to say, "not that kind. I want to stop pretending." But instead he let her put the picture in his hand. A family—father, mother, grandmother, and a little boy—clustered around a table set with gold-rimmed china and wine glasses. From habit, a habit that felt like the crux of his childhood, he'd looked first at the little boy, trying to see if he could remember how it felt to be him. The boy held a forkful of mashed potatoes to his lips; he wore a tie and navy blazer and his hair had been slicked back from his forehead. The tilt of his head and the smooth sweep of his hair made him look like a child who had spent his childhood being fussed over by adults who loved him. The desire to be him, to take that as his own memory, tugged at Toby.

Holding up a microscope slide, he shrugged away from Julie's reaching hand. "I need to run this through the processor," he said, already rolling his stool away from her.

In the weeks that followed he called his mother often, blocking his number so she wouldn't know it was him. She always picked up, no matter what time he called. "Hello," she would say, "who's this?"

He never answered her. The sound of her breath through the phone, a sound like the surge of the ocean, made him feel as if he held a seashell to his ear. He'd grown up attuned to his mother's breath, its rhythm a barometer that allowed him to measure her happiness. The regular exhalations he heard through the phone comforted him.

After his father left, he'd been afraid that his mother would leave too. Not yet in kindergarten, small enough to wake frightened and crying in the middle of the night, he would sob her name into the darkness of his bedroom. The teacups of crème de menthe she sipped in the evenings made her sleep so deeply that she never heard him. The distance from his bed to where she slept across the hall seemed insurmountable. Through the open doors of their bedrooms he could hear her moaning breaths choke into silence before ending in a trailing whimper.

"Don't be sad," his mother had said when he tried to tell her about the nights when he couldn't sleep. "When you're sad, I'm sad too. There's nothing we need to be sad about. Let's make ourselves some happy memories, OK?" Because he loved his mother, he did what she asked.

He had never been talkative, but that fall he enclosed himself in silence. The other lab techs grew into the habit of talking around him. "Half an hour until my break," they would say, or "Have you tried Rachael Ray's recipe for chorizo-cheese waffles?" They taped pictures of their children and their dogs to the insides of cabinet doors and marked calendars with upcoming vacations and birthdays. Every Friday they collected money for the Powerball office pool and chatted about the houses they would live in and the vacations they would take if they won. He no longer participated. The future felt as changeable and uncertain as water, the past as precarious as a fault line. Only the present moment felt secure enough to trust, but memory moved in him like a snake, slithering at the edge of his consciousness, flexing and looping its muscular coils. He fought its constriction and the effort exhausted him.

One day early in December he added Giemsa stain to a blood sample, then placed the slide beneath a microscope. Healthy pink cells the size of lentils filled his field of vision, but as he scanned across the slide he discovered a cluster of blastoma cells lurking at the edge. The cells had expanded into swollen rounds with deep purple nuclei and transparent, misshapen margins. In the center of each cell a structure like a snail shell curled back on itself.

"Remember our Thanksgiving that year?" his mother had said on that day in the garage. "Remember when Grandma Zelda said she'd never seen a little boy eat that much? See how happy we look?" She'd leaned in close to look at the picture with him.

The cells blurred as his fingers tightened on the focusing knob at the side of the microscope. He adjusted the eyepiece and increased the light intensity until the glare reflecting off the slide made him blink.

There had never been a Grandma Zelda, only his mother's stories about her, stories that changed depending on his mother's mood. There had never been a Thanksgiving, either, at least not like the one she wanted him to remember. In the picture silver bowls of Brussels sprouts and cranberry sauce stood next to a basket of bread rolls. Prices and descriptions of the furniture and tableware were printed across the bottom of the picture; the crystal drop chandelier was on sale for $539. Their Thanksgivings had been just the two of them, celebrated with TV dinners in foil trays: slices of turkey and gravy in the largest compartment, mashed potatoes and peas in triangles to either side, and a rectangle of cinnamon stewed apples.

The man in the picture stood at the head of the table, a carving knife poised above a glistening turkey. His mother had glued a photo of her face onto the man's body. It was an old photo, taken when her hair was still red-blonde, before she started scraping the brittle, fading strands into a knot at the back of her head. She'd used small, precise cuts to trim the photo so that her hair curled around the man's shoulders.

He took the slide off the microscope platform. Without the magnifying lens, the chemical stain made a uniform pink smear across the slide, revealing no difference between the healthy and unhealthy cells. When he set the slide back in its tray, it left behind grooves in his skin where he had gripped too tightly.

"Oops." His mother had tugged the Thanksgiving picture away from him. "It's not quite finished yet." Another photo of her face rested in her palm. "We just need to glue this on." She handed him a bottle of glue and pointed to the mother in the picture. "Put it there. Then we'll find a face for you. Unless you like that face? Do you want to keep that one?"

The boy in the picture smirked at Toby from behind his forkful of mashed potatoes.

Toby's hands left sweaty prints on the metal countertop beside the microscope. He picked up the tray of slides and it rattled in his grasp. Julie glanced over from where she stood in front of the centrifuge. Her lips moved, but he couldn't hear what she was saying through the ringing in his ears.

"I think I'm sick," he whispered. "I need to go home." He set the slides on the counter and walked out of the room.

"This isn't my memory," he had said to his mother. "I don't want to pretend anymore." The words felt like stones dredged from a silted riverbed. "I want something real." He took the picture from her and crumpled it before throwing it into the wastebasket.

Vinyl tiles in a checkerboard of beige and brown covered the corridor floor. He stepped from tile to tile until he reached the exit. When he pushed through the door, cold air swirled around him. Needles of snow pricked his face. He walked along a row of parked cars to the far corner of the lot where his own car sat. Thick, gray light filtered through the clouds. A crust of ice cracked beneath his fingers when he lifted the door handle. He crawled in and pulled the door closed behind him.

"Why haven't you ever given me a picture of my father?" he had asked on that day in the garage. "I don't want to be afraid anymore of making you unhappy. I want my real memories." He reached for the metal box of photos on the table.

"She's not ours," he said, holding up a black-and-white oval portrait of a woman with her hair pinned on top of her head and a cameo at her throat. "Not ours," he said as he showed her a 4 x 6 snapshot of a young man displaying a fish the length of his forearm. He threw them onto her lap, then upended the box. Photos scattered around them, a crowd of strangers that his mother had adopted. He turned over the photo that had fallen nearest to him. A younger version of his mother looked back at him, her mouth stretched into the smile of someone who has been told to look happy but can't quite remember what that might look like. She held the hand of a toddler. Part of the photo had been ripped away. One of the boy's arms reached toward the missing part of the photo. His hand and forearm had been torn off.

"That's me," he said.

She took the photo from him and touched the ragged edge the way one might touch a wound. He felt dizzy with the sense that he was rushing toward something he didn't want to know. The garage smelled sour, like spoiled milk and old paper, a smell that he recognized from his childhood. He couldn't remember what it had felt like to be that child, couldn't remember any stories to go with the hope in the boy's face as he looked up at his mother. His skin felt as if he'd been stung by a swarm of wasps. He watched her slide the photo into the pocket of her cardigan. The gentle way she folded the wool around the photo told him that she still remembered what it felt like to be the woman in the photo.

"That's not one of our stories," she said. Her skin looked translucent, a covering too fragile to protect her from his need to remember.

She took the crumpled Thanksgiving collage from the wastebasket. "Remember when," she said as she smoothed the creases from the picture. Her cuticles were raw and swollen. She held the picture out to him, but it was upside down. "Remember when," she said again. He turned and ran, dodging around the stacked boxes. When he emerged from the garage, the cold rain on his skin had felt like grief.

Snowflakes drifted onto the windshield. The fine, hard snow that had stung him as he walked through the parking lot had unfurled into something softer and thicker. He climbed out of his car and stretched his arms out to catch the flakes on his shirtsleeves. Feathers of ice radiated from the center of each crystal, melting quickly in the warmth of his breath. He touched his face with clumsy, cold-stiffened fingers to confirm the tears on his cheeks.

The next morning he woke up early to leave a voice mail for the lab director. "I won't be in today," he said. "I'm not feeling well." The upward inflection of his voice made it a question. He held the phone to his cheek for a moment after disconnecting the call.

Three stories below, cars idled in the McDonald's drive-through lane. During the night snowplows had churned the snow into piles of gray slush along the curbs.

From habit he padded into the kitchen, a narrow galley separated from his bedroom by a half-wall of particleboard cabinets. A banana peel slumped across the countertop next to a scattering of bread crumbs. He opened the silverware drawer and tested the weight of a fork, then pressed his thumb into the curved bowl of a spoon. Salad forks, dinner forks, teaspoons, tablespoons, and butter knives nested in a compartmentalized tray—a matched set with handles like flattened teardrops. His mother's silverware drawer jumbled tarnished silver and plastic picnic ware with blunted paring knives and chopsticks still in their red paper wrappings. He watched his hands touch the utensils. A pad of muscle bulged at the base of his thumb. Pale, sparse hair sprouted on his knuckles. His fingers plucked at the stack of teaspoons, then slid along the flat length of a butter knife.

He still kept his father in the soft places beneath his skin. Shards of memory like splintered glass hid inside him—the sudden slam of a door, the grip of a hand dusted with freckles, the rasp of a voice raised in anger. For years the sound of his mother's small, suffocating gasps or a glimpse of the mushroom-like pouches beneath her eyes had caused the splinters to burrow deeper into the shelter of his body. Better the thousand cuts of a fractured memory than the burden of adding to his mother's sadness.

He closed the silverware drawer and went back to his bedroom. The twist of sheet and blankets on his bed looked like a shucked cocoon. He tucked himself into the cocoon with the care one gives a child. The folds of wool and cotton beneath his chin smelled oily and private, like the creases of his mother's skin.

His father had broken his arm. The truth of it sat on his tongue like a pearl. After the cast came off, his mother had rubbed lotion into the flaking, itchy skin on his arm every night. He had been afraid to touch his arm. The capacity of his body to break felt like a betrayal, one that could be dealt with only by disowning the broken part of himself. One night his mother took a Matchbox car and ran it up and down his arm, then brought the car to a halt on top of the healing scar. After she tucked him in and left the room he took the car from his nightstand and rolled it across his arm, slowly at first, then faster and faster as the sound of his father's footsteps moved from the living room to the kitchen and up the stairs to pause outside his bedroom. Peeking through his eyelashes, he'd seen his father in the doorway, a dark outline inside a rectangle of light. He'd wanted his father to come in and say good night to him, wanted it with an intensity that left a sour taste in his mouth, but when his father turned away without speaking, he'd been relieved. After his father disappeared into his parents' bedroom across the hall, he'd pressed his fingers into the place where his arm had broken, hoping for the sharpness of pain, but finding only a dull ache.

The next morning his father was gone. When he got up, his mother pulled him onto her lap. "Let me tell you a happy story," she'd said. He'd pretended not to notice that she was crying.

Beneath the reassuring weight of the blankets, he probed the tendons and muscle of his forearm until he found a line of scar tissue the length of a Matchbox car. The underlying bone felt solid, like something impossible to break.

For days and then weeks he tried to understand himself as a person whose father had broken his arm and disappeared without saying goodbye. The world felt inverted, like a photographer's negative, shadows lit bright so that he noticed things he hadn't before. He watched a senior lab technician's fingers skim across the picture of his divorced wife that he kept inside his locker. Working shoulder to shoulder with Julie at the tissue processing station, he saw her lips move in a silent prayer, a prayer that started with the word "goddamnit," every time she labeled the slides of a child with leukemia. He noticed how one of the phlebotomists avoided speaking her son's name, referring to him as "boy," as in "the boy is back in rehab again."

"What's his name?" he asked, frightened by the ease with which the phlebotomist had made her son into a stranger. He thought she wasn't going to answer. When she did, she spoke her son's name like a word that had to be held safe in her mouth.

He felt porous, formed around absence, like the fist-sized chunk of white coral his mother bought for him the year he turned six. When she found it at a thrift store, she turned it over to show him the honeycombed hollows within its pitted skeleton. "Remember when we snorkeled the Great Barrier Reef?" she asked. He had thought of blue water and sunlight so hot that it hurt his skin, a sensation that became inseparable from the memory of his mother reading aloud the Australia pages in his *Children's Encyclopedia*.

Sometimes he woke in the middle of the night from a dream in which his father waited for him just outside his bedroom. He could see a path through his memory to a place where he held out his arms and his father moved from the doorway into the bedroom. "I'm going away," his father would have said, "because I love you so much and I don't want to hurt you again." Denying himself the comfort of this revised memory hurt so much that he pounded his thighs with his fists. For much of January and February a garden of bruises bloomed across his thighs: ruddy, swollen skin layered atop deepening purples and faded greens.

At the beginning of March a three-day rainstorm washed away the last hard ridges of snow lingering at the edge of the lab parking lot. He stopped dreaming of his father and instead lay awake thinking about his mother, imagining the ocean of her breath rising and falling.

He filled out a March Madness bracket and put five dollars in the office pool. He wanted to call his mother and didn't.

"I haven't spoken to my mother for five months," he told Julie. "I never wanted to hurt her. I don't know how to fix the last five months."

"You can't erase what's already happened," she said. "You can only change the future."

He draped a translucent slice of tissue across a glass slide, taking care to lay it flat and smooth. Formaldehyde stung his nose, blending with the raw odor of blood and tissue. When Julie's hand settled on his shoulder, he leaned into the comfort of it.

After his shift was over, he turned right out of the parking lot instead of left, taking a road that led him to the interstate. Miles slipped by, measured in incremental changes of light, until the cold shell of starlit sky above the highway made him reach for reassurance in the solidity of the windshield and door panels enclosing him. When he arrived at his mother's house, he pulled into the driveway. His headlights illuminated the garage burrowed into the hillside beneath the house. The garage window radiated a weak, yellow light. He turned off the headlights, then the engine. Above him the house slumped into its foundation, windows dark and empty. The front porch slanted toward the tangled thistles edging the front door, their tough roots preventing a further downward slide to the road below.

He stepped out of his car and moved toward the garage. A breath of cold wind brushed his skin as he peered into the window. A shadowed tower of boxes blocked his view. Webs of spider silk clung to his fingers where he touched the windowsill. When he tried the knob on the side door, it turned freely, but the effort of opening the door and stepping inside felt like pushing against the current of a river during flood season.

"Mom?" He heard his own vulnerability, his need for her to be someone he could love. "Mom?" Despite his attempt to deepen his voice it remained the sound of a little boy seeking his mother.

"Toby? Is that you?"

The fearful hope in the way she said his name reminded him of all the times he'd called out for her as a child and she'd answered. He moved deeper into the cluttered space. A torn quilt draped over a treadle sewing machine. Yellow rubber boots peeked out of the top of a plastic bin filled with extension cords. He found her at the back of the garage, seated at her worktable.

"It's me," he said.

The soft, blue shadows beneath her eyes told him that her dreams were no easier than his own. The skin on her forearms drooped, as if there wasn't enough of her to fill the outline of herself. When she saw him looking at the table, she folded her arms over the picture in front of her.

He stepped closer. "It's OK," he said. He tugged the picture of a snow-covered mountain out from beneath her arms. A ragged edge showed where she'd ripped it from a magazine. The flimsy paper was mounted on a piece of cardboard. Two stick figures sketched in shaky, penciled lines climbed up the mountainside.

"Is that us?" he asked.

Her fingertips skimmed over her arms as if checking to make sure that she hadn't disappeared. "It could be," she said. "If you wanted it to be."

The cut-out faces of young men and boys covered the table. He reached out and touched the ruddy-cheeked face of a boy who looked like he climbed mountains every day before breakfast. "Not that one," he said. "Not any of these." He reached for the box of photos. "Let's use my real face." He sifted through the photos, searching all the way to the bottom of the box to find the ripped photo of himself as a toddler, the one he'd found all those months ago.

"This one." He held it out to her.

She pulled her sweater more tightly around herself. "That's from a sad time," she said, speaking as if the words themselves hurt her. "Let's find a happier one."

"I like this one." He bent over the table and picked up the X-acto knife. "Remember when we climbed the mountain?" he asked as he trimmed his face from the photo. "I didn't know if we'd make it, but you kept going and you took me with you." He put a dot of glue on the back of the face and attached it to the smaller stick figure. "Now we just need to find a face for you."

He looked down at the photo beneath his fingers. His mother's face looked back at him, still trapped in a past she couldn't escape. "We could use this one if you want," he said. "But it's only part of the story, not all of it. The way I remember it, there were times on the mountain when we felt sad, but also times when we were happy."

She took the old photo from him and cradled it in her hands, as if her touch could reach back through time to comfort her younger self. "Do you think we made it to the top of the mountain?" she asked.

He looked down at the two angular figures leaning into the mountain, marching up-wards with skinny, reaching legs. His hopeful face looked toward the peak, toward the mother climbing above him, pulling him along behind her. A "yes" waited on his tongue. He held it there inside his mouth, lingering in the moment of arrival.

Disabled, Queer Pride and Kinship in *Laura Hershey: On the Life and Work of an American Master*

Meg Day and Niki Herd, eds. *Laura Hershey: On the Life and Work of an American Master*. Warrensburg, MO: Pleiades Press, 2019. 249 pp. $16. Softcover.

The title of the latest installment of Pleiades Press' Unsung Masters series, *Laura Hershey: On the Life and Work of an American Master,* reveals one important aspect of Hershey's work: that she is, unquestionably, a master of American poetry. The cover, featuring Hershey beaming at the camera from her wheelchair, centers Hershey as a poet of disability, but it's only in reading the anthology itself that one gets a true sense of the power of her poetry. This anthology is not *just* about Laura Hershey but also about the strands of queer and disabled kinship that endure through her poetry and her activism.

"As is so often the case when we come up without access to our own lineages, I knew little of Laura Hershey's life, the expansiveness of it, and the great extent to which the work she'd done in the world had made much of my life—especially my education—possible," co-editor Meg Day writes of her friend in her tender and eloquent introduction. Day, Eli Clare, and several other contributors to the collection shared a direct kinship with Hershey, but even those who didn't know Hershey directly write about her with the reverence of a foremother. "I didn't know Hershey," Leah Lakshmi Piepzna-Samarasinha writes in an essay. "I didn't know who she was or her two decades of disabled queer radical literary and political work. I didn't know a damn thing about her before she died....Disability writers aren't taught, and so even when invested and involved as activists, we miss out on knowing our lineage." Though Piepzna-Samarasinha never knew Hershey before her death, that both she and Day recognize Hershey as an elder speaks to the intense difficulty inherent in establishing a poetic lineage of disabled poets, a difficulty that this anthology begins to correct.

Accessibility is, fittingly, one of the dominant themes throughout the book, appearing over and over not only in the poems themselves but in the anthology's extensive section of critical essays about Hershey. Though all her poems prioritize access and inclusiveness, I think the best example is her stunning ars poetica "How to Write a Poem," which opens:

> Don't be brilliant.
> Don't use words for their own sake, or to show
> how clever you are,
> how thoroughly you have subjugated them
> to your will, the words.
>
> Don't try to write a poem
> as good as your favorite poet.
> Don't even try to write
> a good poem.
>
> Just peel back the folds over your heart
> and shine into it
> the strongest light that streams
> from your eyes, or somewhere else. (64)

The poem not only reveals the foundational principles undergirding Hershey's style, but also serves as a thesis statement for the anthology itself. Her poems compel their audience to remember that language can be—and often is—a form of subjugation, and urge writers to prioritize candor over style. As a result, her poems are fearless in their straightforwardness, relentlessly accessible in the proudest, most valiant sense of the word.

"Self-indulgence, cockiness, and ambition have no place in Hershey's aesthetic," Constance Merritt observes in her discussion of "How to Write a Poem." Unlike so many other poets, Hershey's work eschews ableist language by embracing bodies' difference: "Bless you, Laura Hershey, for the inclusiveness of 'or somewhere else,'" Merritt writes. "Light may come from the eyes, but it may also come from somewhere else. Wherever it comes from, again Hershey insists that illumination is one of poetry's most vital means and ends....[P]oetry is not a vehicle for your ambition, but *rather it shapes itself only* to the poet's need."

Emotional need is hardly Hershey's primary concern, however, and many of the poems are, as Day puts it, "thrillingly queer; they allow the personal to be political while still finding ways to separate the two when desire demands it." That so many of these poems embrace desire from a disabled perspective would be radical enough, but to embrace disability and queerness simultaneously gives writers who are both disabled *and* queer an even more specific—and crucial—form of permission.

Hershey's poems show a younger generation of disabled queer writers that it is not only possible to have serious relationships, as Hershey did with lawyer and fellow disability activist Robin Stevens, but flings, too, as she illustrates in the delightfully wry poem, "Progress." In this poem, Hershey writes about a woman who "was interested, / romantically—she wanted me / to know. But"—and then comes a myriad of excuses, that Hershey is "in a wheelchair, and hardly / able to move," that "in relationships she was never / the aggressor," and (most flimsy of all) that she "feared having me grow / to depend on her." Hershey answers each of these excuses in turn with a poem which she summarizes for us, but once the beloved finally admits that "she doesn't know," Hershey's speaker, exasperated, closes the poem by demanding, "Someday I'll ask her / no paper between us / Girl, when you gonna get your shit together / so we can have this fling?" The speaker's frustration at the potential lover for failing to "get her shit together" places the onus squarely where it belongs: on the potential lover's ableism. The fact that the beloved can't see Hershey as a viable sexual partner comes down to her own failure of imagination, not any limitations of Hershey's body.

This is not to say, however, that Hershey does not also write about limitations. She does, though she is always conscious that these limitations are a facet of the world around her, rather than a failing of her own body. In "A Day," the only poem in the anthology directly addressed to her partner, Robin Stevens, Hershey longs to give her partner a glimpse of "the future / we hope we are building." The love poem combines its own inherent queerness with an architecture of disabled futurism, where there are

> no demonstrations to prepare for,
> because justice demonstrates itself these days;
> no meetings,
> which have mostly been replaced
> by simple understanding;
> not even a conference to attend,
> because issues like caregiver abuse
> and work disincentives
> were settled long ago. (169)

The poem is both optimistic and bittersweet, in that it projects Hershey and her beloved into a future that would never exist in the poet's lifetime yet dares to imagine it anyway. In this poem, and in so many others, Hershey calls this future into existence by writing down what she wants that future to be.

There's something spell-like about the way she crafts her language, and it often really *does* feel as if Hershey can conjure up a lover, or an access ramp, through the sheer force of her desire (or perhaps because, as she notes in her poem "Hate, But," "as it happens, I am a witch"). Anaphora and refrain are two hallmarks of her style that give her poems this spell-like feel. Perhaps her most famous refrain, "you get proud / by practicing," presents itself clearest, as it appears in several of the essays on Hershey's work. But what I love most about this devotion to refrain is not only its musicality but its insistence, for Hershey is not only a poet of disability, of queerness, of womanhood, but also a poet of insistence. Over and over, Hershey's work lays undeniable claim to her rights, to her body, to her space, to her joy and, by extension, the rights, body, space, and joy of all of her disabled and/or queer kin.

Nothing about us without us, Hershey's poems insist. *We're here.* And, like Hershey's work, we're here to stay.

The Dark Heart of Florida: Jon Sealy's *The Edge of America*

Jon Sealy. *The Edge of America*. Richmond, VA: Haywire Books, 2019. 293 pp. $17.95.Softcover.

At the beginning of this tautly plotted, atmospheric crime noir novel, Jon Sealy quotes Joseph Conrad in an epigraph: "If I had the necessary talent I would like to go for the true anarchist—which is the millionaire. Then you would see the venom flow." This tremendously intelligent and expansive novel goes on to fulfill Conrad's aspiration in the largest sense by examining the mercurial political and financial systems of America that make money for those who are already rich.

Like Conrad's *Heart of Darkness*, *The Edge of America* is set in an era when the majority of people don't question the savage behaviors of those who make money for them. Instead of imperialist England and the Belgian Congo, the increasingly dark events of Sealy's novel take place in the mid-1980s, in sunny southern Florida, "a state on the edge, an appendage isolated from the rest of America." Told through alternating points of view, it recounts the story of Bobby West, an executive of a holdings company whose legitimate investments—boat shops, gun shops, travel and real estate agencies—serve as a front for CIA surveillance in Florida. When a local gangster named Alexander French lures him into a money-laundering racket, West drifts easily into the scheme. His ill-gotten money comes like a flood. He hides it all in a safe in the floor of his home office. When the money disappears, along with his daughter, Holly, West is forced to wade into a dark underworld peopled by the drug cartel, political operatives, and bankers.

This is Sealy's second novel, the follow-up to *The Whiskey Baron* (Hub City Press, 2014), a crime thriller set in an upstate South Carolina mill town during the Great Depression. In *The Edge of America*, Sealy remains preoccupied with rootless characters doomed because they remain cut off from their communities and their pasts. His characters look to money, rather than religion, to provide consolation during a morally bankrupt time. Bobby West is the perfectly imperfect noir hero. Estranged from his wife and daughter, he vaguely remembers his Midwestern, middle-class upbringing in suburban Illinois, his father's modest goals of owning a home, supporting a family, and remaining out of debt. West considers most people around him to be as hardworking and earnest as his father, which is why West spends his days filling out spreadsheets, hoping Fidel Castro and the Soviets will stir up a world crisis so he can turn a large profit off the political unrest. When Mr. French approaches him with the money-laundering scheme, West muses simply, "Now what else do I have to do besides make money like everyone else in America?" West's indolent daughter, Holly, is equally unmoored. Raised by contentious parents, she has only a tenuous grasp of the present, and no concept of the future. Lacking awareness of who she is and what she's doing with the three million dollars she's stolen from her father, she barely knows the teenage boy, Keith Sorrells, who transports her north in a rental truck stocked with dubious contents by one of Alexander French's henchmen.

In a series of alternating takes that counterpoint the story of Bobby West, Sealy tells Keith's story. A preacher's son from upstate South Carolina, Sorrels holds no nostalgia for home, or for the religion his father proselytizes. He's never heard of the American Dream—at least not in the way West envisions it from his own youth—so he doesn't suffer the loss of it. If anything, he suffers from a lack of imagination, and malaise. He understands only that he wants a pretty girlfriend, a job that pays above minimum wage, and a way out of the small, Christ-haunted backwater town where he was raised. After Holly ditches him, Keith returns home from his journey as a drug mule for Alexander French. Within the sanctuary of his father's church, his father sermonizes that it's not so bad being a transient, that being a seeker is the mark of a holy man, and the word "holy" means "set apart."

Sealy revels in atmospheric descriptions of cities and rural routes that emphasize the transience and isolation of his characters. He creates rich and shifting settings that echo the book's noir ambivalence between the America most people want to see and its seedy underbelly. Outside the glamour of Miami's Art Deco District, transplanted palm trees and hibiscus barely camouflage the tacky tourist scene, "a boozy blur of bright lights and colorful clothing and loud music." Southern Florida is the edge of America, but also the languid heart from which the affluent "me-first" 1980s mind-set radiates. Sealy is equally adept at depicting every seedy establishment along the highways of rural America. While fleeing Miami, West's daughter, Holly, stops at a gas station in rural Georgia with hopes of finding a shower. As she wanders through the convenience store, surveying rows of cheap beer, rebel flags, and an astonishing variety of beef jerky, it becomes clear that the transients who drive the rural highways of America aren't holy, or even innocent; they're just wayward children who want the relative safety afforded by the food aisles in a truck stop.

Ultimately, Sealy uses these noir elements to frame the story, transmuting this book into a more expansive meditation upon a time when American culture began to reward those who gamed the system more than it rewarded hard work and integrity. Drug runners, political operatives, and one Russian assassin haunt the periphery of the central action, but the real villains implicated by this novel are the politicians, banks and big businesses that capitalize on those who become anesthetized by money and the hope of making more of it. As the darker forces encroach upon West, he surmises, "Money was the real drug of the United States of America." Though his central characters remain dimly aware of this new reality, Sealy offers his readers a clear-eyed and unflinching vision of the American Dream on the verge of unraveling.

SCR

Not Only on Sundays

Like a cleric's cassock,
evening folds up all doubt
in the outback
of an uneasy America,

where a cast of parishioners
cast their lot with the spirit
of settlers once nurtured
on frontiers

by circuit riders,
who blessed, saved,
and buried them
any day of the week.

Along with publication of Dr. Ron Moran's poem "Not Only on Sundays," the editors of *The South Carolina Review* are pleased to announce the establishment of The Ronald Moran Prize in Fiction and Poetry, which will be awarded annually to one poet and one fiction writer appearing in that year's volume of *SCR* (beginning with issues 52:1 and 52:2). All contributors with no more than one published volume of fiction or poetry will be eligible for the $250 prize. The winners will be selected by the *SCR* editorial staff.

We thank Dr. Moran for his generosity in establishing this prize, and we appreciate his ongoing contributions to both *SCR* (in which he has published many poems over the years) and to Clemson University, where he taught for over thirty years and served as both English Department Chair and Dean of the College of Architecture, Arts, and Humanities (see Dr. Moran's full bio in the contributors' notes).

CONTRIBUTORS

O-JEREMIAH AGBAAKIN holds an LL.B from the University of Ibadan. His poems are forthcoming/published in *Puerto del Sol*, *West Branch*, *Pittsburgh Poetry Journal*, *Poetry Northwest*, *Notre Dame Review*, *RATTLE* and elsewhere. He reads for *PANK Magazine*.

LEVI ANDALOU's work has appeared or is forthcoming in *Mid-American Review*, *The Minnesota Review*, *Lake Effect*, *Spillway*, *BOMB*, *Virga Magazine*, *Sugar House Review*, *DIAGRAM*, *F(r)iction*, *Cleaver Magazine*, *Sonora Review*, *Phoebe*, *Ruminate*, *Pembroke Magazine*, and *Tampa Review*. He was a finalist for both the 2018 Greg Grummer Poetry Award and the 2018 *Puerto Del Sol* Poetry Contest, and a semifinalist for the 2018 *Boulevard* Emerging Poets Contest. In 2019, he was nominated by *Pembroke Magazine* for inclusion in the Best New Poets anthology series. He graduated from Brown University, where he studied with C.D. Wright, Michael S. Harper, and Ange Mlinko. He lives in the San Francisco Bay Area. Read more of his work or contact him at LeviAndalou.com.

DEAN BAKOPOULOS is the author of three novels, including *Please Don't Come Back from the Moon*, a *New York Times* Notable Book; he also co-wrote the film adaptation, which debuted at the 2017 Los Angeles Film Festival. The recipient of a Guggenheim Fellowship and two National Endowment for the Arts fellowships, he is currently writer-in-residence at Grinnell College and teaches in the Warren Wilson MFA Program. Along with his spouse and writing partner, Alissa Nutting, he is currently developing several television projects, including the forthcoming series *Made for Love*.

CAROLINE PARKMAN BARR is a north Alabama native and a graduate of the MFA Writing Program at the University of North Carolina at Greensboro, where she served as Poetry Editor of *The Greensboro Review*. Her poetry has appeared or is forthcoming in *RHINO*, *North Dakota Quarterly*, *Connotation Press*, and elsewhere. She is currently the Social Media Specialist for *Poetry Northwest*.

DAVID BLAIR is the author of three books of poetry: *Ascension Days*, *Friends with Dogs*, and *Arsonville*. He is also the author of *Walk Around: Essays on Poetry and Place* and a forthcoming poetry collection, *Barbarian Seasons*, both from MadHat Press. Learn more about him and his work at davidblairpoetry.com.

ANTHONY BORRUSO has an MFA in creative writing from Butler University and has been a reader for *Booth: A Journal*. Currently, he teaches composition at Tallahassee Community College. His poems have been published or are forthcoming in *The American Journal of Poetry*, *Spillway*, *Mantis*, *THRUSH*, and elsewhere.

HILARY BROWN is a Pushcart-nominated poet and activist living in Oakland, California. Their chapbook, *When She Woke She Was an Open Field*, is available from Headmistress Press and their work can be found in *Queerly*, *The Ocotillo Review*, and *Apt* among other publications.

EMILY ROSE COLE is the author of *Love & a Loaded Gun*, a chapbook of persona poems in the voices of mythological and historical women (Minerva Rising Press, 2017). She has received awards from *Jabberwock Review*, *Philadelphia Stories*, *The Orison Anthology*, and the Academy of American Poets. Her poetry has appeared or is forthcoming in *American Life in Poetry*, *Best New Poets 2018*, *Carve*, and *River Styx*, among others. She holds an MFA from Southern Illinois University Carbondale and is a PhD candidate in Poetry and Disability Studies at the University of Cincinnati, where she is a Taft Fellow. Find her at emilyrosecolepoetry.com.

EMILY COLLINS's work has appeared or is forthcoming in *Oyster River Pages*, *The Chicago Review of Books*, *Coal Hill Review*, *The McNeese Review*, *Entropy*, and others. She lives in Portland, Maine.

HOLLY DAY's poetry has recently appeared in *Asimov's Science Fiction*, *Grain*, and *The Tampa Review*. Her newest poetry collections are *In This Place, She Is Her Own* (Vegetarian Alcoholic Press), *A Wall to Protect Your Eyes* (Pski's Porch Publishing), *Folios of Dried Flowers and Pressed Birds* (Cyberwit.net), *Where We Went Wrong* (Clare Songbirds Publishing), *Into the Cracks* (Golden Antelope Press), and *Cross Referencing a Book of Summer* (Silver Bow Publishing).

Born and raised in Georgia, **MONIC DUCTAN** now lives in Tennessee, where she is an assistant professor at Tennessee Tech University. Monic's writing has appeared in numerous literary journals, including *Shenandoah, Water~Stone Review, Tahoma Literary Review, Big Muddy, storySouth,* and *Arkansas Review.* She is at work on her first novel, a book about a Gullah girl leaving her South Carolina sea island.

MARY GRIMM has published *Left to Themselves* (novel) and *Stealing Time* (story collection), both with Random House. Her stories have been published in *The New Yorker, Antioch Review,* and *Mississippi Review.* She teaches fiction writing at Case Western Reserve University.

CANESE JARBOE is the author of the chapbook *dark acre* (Willow Springs Books, 2018) and their debut poetry collection is forthcoming with YesYes Books in 2020. Their poems have appeared in *Bennington Review, Indiana Review, Willow Springs,* and elsewhere. Canese currently lives and teaches in Louisiana.

BRAD JOHNSON's second book *Smuggling Elephants Through Airport Security* (Michigan State University Press) was selected by Carolyn Forche for the 2018 Wheelbarrow Books Poetry Prize. His work has also been accepted by *Hayden's Ferry Review, J Journal, Meridian, Poet Lore, Salamander, Southern Indiana Review, Tampa Review, Tar River Poetry* and others.

EMILY ALICE KATZ's short fiction has appeared or is forthcoming in *Lilith, Confrontation,* and *Mud Season Review,* among other publications, and has been recognized by *Glimmer Train.* She lives in Durham, North Carolina, with her family. You can read more about her at emilyalicekatz.com.

CINDY KING's work has appeared in *The Sun, Callaloo, North American Review, Crab Orchard Review, Black Warrior Review, Cincinnati Review,* and elsewhere. Her book-length poetry collection, *Zoonotic,* will be published by Tinderbox Editions in 2020. She is an Assistant Professor of Creative Writing at Dixie State University and Faculty Editor of *The Southern Quill.*

MAURICE MANNING's next book, *Railsplitter,* will be published this fall. He lives with his family in Kentucky and teaches at Transylvania University.

RONALD MORAN has published fifteen collections of poetry, two books of criticism (one coauthored), and hundreds of poems, essays, and reviews in a number of journals, including *Connecticut Poetry Review, Commonweal, North American Review, Northwest Review, Southern Poetry Review,* and *Southern Review.* Moran lives in Simpsonville, South Carolina.

CECIL MORRIS, a retired English teacher from Roseville, California, has had poems in *English Journal, American Scholar, Poem, Plainsongs, Hiram Review, Dime Show Review, The 2River Review, Red River Review,* and other literary magazines.

RICK MULKEY is the author of five books and chapbooks, including *Ravenous: New & Selected Poems,* and *Toward Any Darkness.* Previous and current work has appeared or is forthcoming in *The Georgia Review, Poet Lore, Poetry East, Southeast Review, Baltimore Review,* and *Crab Orchard Review.* He currently directs and teaches in the low-residency MFA program at Converse College in South Carolina.

JOHN A. NIEVES has poems forthcoming or recently published in journals such as *North American Review, Poetry Northwest, Southern Review, 32 Poems,* and *Copper Nickel.* He won the *Indiana Review* Poetry Contest, and his first book, *Curio,* won the Elixir Press Annual Poetry Award Judge's Prize. He is associate professor of English at Salisbury University and an editor of *The Shore Poetry.*

LISA RHOADES is the author of *Strange Gravity,* selected by Elaine Terranova for the Bright Hill Press Poetry Award Series and the forthcoming *The Long Grass* (Saint Julian Press, 2020). In addition to teaching, she works as a pediatric nurse. She lives on Staten Island with her spouse and their two children. Follow her at lisarhoades.com.

JOSÉ SOTOLONGO was born in Cuba. His fiction has appeared in numerous magazines and has been nominated for the Pushcart Prize. His novel, *The Scented Chrysalis,* was released in 2019 from Adelaide Books. He lives with his husband in the Catskills of New York.

NATHAN SPOON is an autistic poet with learning disabilities and "low academic fluency" whose poems have appeared in the publications *Poetry, Mantis, Harvard Divinity Bulletin, The Scores, Oxford Poetry,* and elsewhere. His debut collection, *Doomsday Bunker,* was published in 2017. He is senior editor of *X-Peri* and a 2019 visiting poet to the Ruth Stone Foundation Reading Series.

SUSAN TEKULVE's newest book, *Second Shift: Essays*, was published by Del Sol Press in 2018. She's also the author of *In the Garden of Stone*, winner of the 2012 South Carolina Novel Prize and a 2014 Gold IPPY Award. She's also published two short story collections: *Savage Pilgrims* and *My Mother's War Stories*. Her nonfiction, short stories, and poems have appeared in journals such as *The Georgia Review*, *The South Carolina Review*, *Connecticut Review*, *The Louisville Review*, *Puerto del Sol*, *New Letters*, and *Shenandoah*. She teaches in the BFA and MFA writing programs at Converse College.

MATTHEW TURBEVILLE is a long-time resident of South Carolina, and has studied writing under some of the greatest writers living today. He has been published in *LitHub/CrimeReads*, *Writers Tell All*, the *Hard Work*, *MysteryPeople*, *BookRiot*, and has worked for *Publishers Weekly*. He is currently at work on his first novel.

SARA WALLACE is the author of *The Rival* and the chapbook *Edge*. Her poetry has appeared in such publications as *Yale Review*, *Agni*, *Hanging Loose*, *Michigan Quarterly Review*, *Poetry Daily* and others. She lives in Brooklyn.

DIANE R. WIENER's first full-length poetry collection, *The Golem Verses*, was published in June, 2018, by Nine Mile Press in LaFayette, New York. Her poems appear in *Nine Mile*, *Wordgathering*, *Tammy*, the *South Carolina Review*, and elsewhere; she has flash fiction in *Ordinary Madness* (Weasel Press). A Research Professor at Syracuse University, Diane has published works on disability justice, pedagogy, and empowerment.

EVANGELINE WRIGHT's fiction has appeared or is forthcoming in *Reckoning, Gone Lawn, Ghost Parachute* and elsewhere. She holds an MFA in Creative Writing from the Vermont College of Fine Arts.

Lightning Source UK Ltd.
Milton Keynes UK
UKHW031920011119
352759UK00005B/79/P